DOWNH

A Scrapbook of Peop

This compendium of fact, fi
has been described as 'All you wanted to know about Downhill but didn't know whom to ask'. It draws together information from many sources to give a picture of the man who built Downhill, his workmen, his relatives, and the subsequent owners of the house, as well as of the grounds and country in which it is placed.

A Roman head
from the Downhill 'marbles'.

DOWNHILL

A Scrapbook of People and Place

Edited from the notebooks of

MISS JAN ECCLES

with an Introduction by

JOHN COLE

LONDON

Printing Ideas & Graphics

1996

First published in 1996
by Printing Ideas & Graphics
84 Calbourne Road, London SW12 8LR

Printed in Great Britain
at The Bath Press, Avon

ISBN: 0 9527486 0 6

Contents

Introduction

This book is a labour of love. Anyone who has met Jan Eccles, during her long and remarkably creative period as curator of the grounds and plants around Downhill, will know that. Others will find it out as they read this book. She would talk so enthusiatically, about all the projects and plans she had for enhancing still further the beauty of an already beautiful place, that a visitor could not avoid being infected by her zeal. Many came to see the gardens, and remained to enjoy her redoubtable skills as raconteur and humourist.

Her principal subject in this book is Frederick Hervey, the eighteenth century 'Earl Bishop' (Bishop of Derry and fourth Earl of Bristol), who created Downhill. He was a prodigious man, with a Renaissance-like range of interests. He was an enthusiastic traveller, and the Bristol hotels in many European cities are called after him. At Downhill, he was a great experimenter in agriculture and horticulture, and introduced many native and exotic trees to his estate.

When the University of Ulster conferred its first honorary Master of Science degree on Jan Eccles in 1983, the Public Orator dropped her a broad hint: 'Some day she might herself produce her own history of Downhill, including in it her voluminous notes and press cuttings, and as yet unrecorded personal memories.' This book fulfils that vision, containing gleanings by Miss Eccles from her scrapbooks.

Jan Eccles' earliest enthusiasm was sailing. She and her brother were brought up by the sea in Sligo, and were inseparable. So when he took up sailing, she was not to be left behind. While he was abroad, one of her earliest solo voyages caused a local furore. She sailed the eight or nine miles to Innismurray Island, then notorious for its poteen production. The islanders had mistaken her for the police, and before they realised their mistake, had dismantled all their illegal stills, and submerged incriminating evidence at the bottom of the sea. This was their common practice when they feared a raid. This probably was the nearest Jan Eccles ever came, inadvertently, to making herself unpopular. She had a soft spot for at least one wrong-doer, an ancestor, John Eccles, who was the last man to be hanged in Omagh. She regards him as misguided, but thinks of him as a Robin Hood, who stole horses, camouflaged them, and gave them to the poor.

Jan Eccles is blessed with a good memory, and she is also a patient listener, with the persistent curiosity usually found only in the young. Her most recent enthusiasm was for the story of a Bonaparte who frequented a hostelry in Magilligan for the sea-bathing.It set her off to find out the truth of a story that Jerome Bonaparte, Napoleon's youngest brother, married the daughter of a Donegal family, Elizabeth Patterson, 'the belle of Baltimore'. Unfortunately, the marriage met with Napoleon Bonaparte's disapproval, since his plans for mastery over Europe included a dynastic marriage for his brother.

Jan Eccles held court for many years in the Gate Lodge of Downhill, where she was warden of the National Trust property. She is now living in retirement in Castlerock. She was already 60 when she took over an overgrown wilderness, and she tended it for 30 years.

Nor were her interests narrowly botanical. She played a key part in the restoration of the Mussenden Temple, that romantic building on the cliff edge, for ever associated with the Earl-Bishop. She also kept a canny eye on the erosion which has affected the cliff itself.

The National Trust is honouring her in an exhibition* which has grown out of another of her enthusiasms: a group of Greek-style statues which had been lost from the original gardens have now been salvaged, and are going on display. Let that exhibition and this book be a celebration of her work at Downhill!

John Cole, May 1995

* At the time of publication this project is as yet unrealised.

Editor's Preface

It will be quickly observed on dipping into these pages that there is very little sequence in the manner of presentation of all this material. We hope that the reader will be indulgent and indeed just *dip*, as our intention has been to retain the notion of a 'scrapbook'. There is an Index and that, combined with cross-references in the body of the text, we hope will help the reader to discover a picture of Downhill, the place and its people.

When selecting material, there are large parts of the original scrapbooks which, of necessity, have not been incorporated, just as there are parts of the original which it was thought required amplification. We make no great claims about original research because most of the information has been obtained from existing sources, and the reader who wishes to follow up any particular points should refer to the Bibliography. However, one of the richest sources of information on almost any Downhill-related subject is the local people, and a visitor to the area will often be well rewarded simply by asking the question.

In a compilation such as this, so very full of dates and details, it is very easy to let an inaccuracy slip through. Like the rector of Desertmartin, the Rev. Robert McGhee, who had the unenviable task of checking the Bishop's account books, we may say that we 'have examined the accounts . . . but yet there may still be errors . . .' and pray that the present reader will be more tolerant than the Bishop.

The Castle, the Bishop's Gate and the waterfall above Drumagully bridge, from the watercolour by Lady Ellen Bruce.

Downhill: the Castle

A VISITOR TODAY, looking at the gaunt ruin of the Castle on the skyline of Downhill, can grasp little of the prodigious feat of its building or be able to imagine how the place might have appeared in its heyday. The Bishop of Derry and Earl of Bristol – of whom much of this scrapbook concerns – never referred to 'sweet Downhill' as the *Palace*, perhaps because properly speaking the Palace was originally Bishop Barnard's official residence in Bishops Street in Derry, and it was our Bishop's home for the first ten years of his incumbency. Occasionally he himself spoke of Downhill as the 'Castle' and it has been so called locally since its building was started.

It is not exactly clear when the building was begun but it can not have been later than 1775 because it was reported to be well under way by the Bishop's friend, Arthur Young, when he passed by in the following year. Young had been to Derry but missed meeting the Bishop there – the Bishop was at that time making a tour of Staffa to compare the volcanic rocks there with those of the Giant's Causeway – and returned 'by Magilligan, for the sake of seeing the shell of the new house building on the sea-coast by the Bishop of Derry which will be a large and convenient edifice when it is finished. It stands on a bold shore where a tree is a rarity.' By the next decade the matter of trees had been dealt with by a vast scheme of planting, though, as can be seen, nothing of that remains now.

Most of what is known of the building of the Castle comes from the records of the accounts and correspondence between the Bishop and the man who became his architect-builder-works-manager and agent, Michael Shanahan (see page 23). Shanahan was from Cork, so it is possible that he met the Bishop when the latter was at Cloyne. Certainly he travelled with the Bishop on the Continent in 1770, acting as tutor to his son, and making geological and architectural drawings. Although many contenders have been suggested for the original design of the Castle, including Wyatt, Cameron and Placido Columbani, it seems possible that Shanahan was mainly responsible even if he drew inspiration from the published copybooks of others. To begin with the house comprised only the south-facing part of what remains today, with its two projecting angled bays and its double flight of curved steps up to the original main entrance. This part of the Castle resembles an unnamed design of Charles Cameron, an architect whose most important work was done in Russia.

From being a comparatively modest 'villa' the Castle soon began to spread, developing first into two long wings which extended northwards. By 1776 over £1,250 had been spent – and paid for – in a mere month's accounting period. The Bishop was not to be so prompt in settling the bills as time went on, and a large part of Shanahan's correspondence concerns money, or rather the lack of it. Much of the rest concerns the problems caused by the Bishop's changes of mind or his infuriating habit of delegating tasks to third parties without apparently consulting his works-manager or indicating what the order of command was to be.

However the great house continued, if erratically. In 1777 'new rooms' were being added and estimates drawn up for stables, coach houses, tack rooms, granary and hayloft as well as for a scullery, larder, dairy, laundry rooms and kitchen. By 1778 a tax was being paid on three hearths and a demesne wall was under way, although Shanahan writes such a long list of works as yet uncompleted that one suspects he wished to keep his changeably minded patron from moving in for at least another half year, adding, significantly, 'as the entire work is elegant it is consequently expensive and tedious', as well as the usual plea for further cash in hand. Also by this time setbacks, misunderstandings and rivalries were setting in:

> 'I cannot see any material advantage that would Accrue by removing the Gibbet doors of the parlour and drawing room from where the[y] stand immediately to the Contrary side of the chimney – such an alteration will for ever put it out of your power to close the Gallery, I would be glad to have this matter finally determined as neither these can be finished until then – as soon as I conveniently can I will send your Lordship my design for the pavilions, I have no Notion of Vieing with your Italian Architects in this respect, I hope to adapt mine to the situation & climate.'

The scathing reference to 'Italian Architects' designs for 'pavilions' is obscure, but it indicates just the kind of complication the Bishop was capable of causing. The designs referred to may have been those

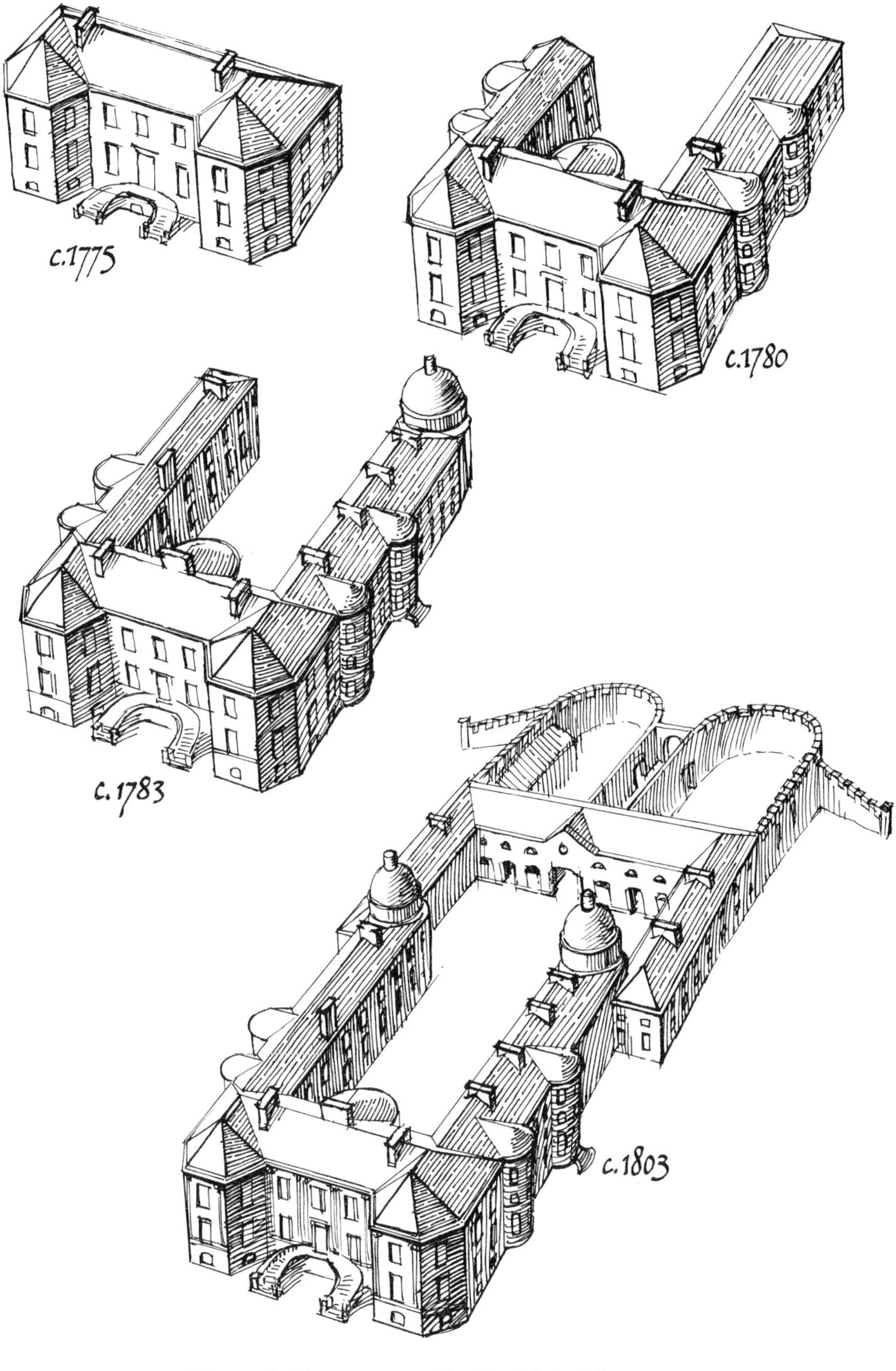

The probable sequence of the Castle's building.

of John Soane (see page 28) or even Placido Columbani. Soane actually came to the site for three fruitless months of 1780, whereas Columbani, who probably came in 1783, seems to have remained for two years and was responsible for overseeing the work and may have had charge of all the internal decoration. Others to arrive were the McBlains, father and son stone masons who had been working on the spire for Derry's cathedral.

The east wing was the first to go up; it contained various rooms and offices and what was later to be called the Curates' Corridor. The gallery of the west wing followed and went through several vicissitudes despite, or even because of, the Bishop's stay in the house during 1779. The height of the ceiling seems to have been one of the most contentious issues, no doubt because the Bishop continued to collect statuary and pictures for the gallery and constantly required yet more space. April of 1783 was a bad month for Shanahan and his letters reached a crescendo of exasperation; 'Your Lordship's letter: this letter with its multiplicity of queries, is merely calculated to puzzle and embarrass my thoughts . . . I have neither the leisure, time nor talents to answer such queries. No man but an adept in the law is equal to such a task.' Then followed another letter seething with pique about Dr Barnard and Mr Loutch's attempts to install a painting (an oil copy of Guido Reni's 'Aurora') in the ceiling of the gallery, apparently with the Bishop's sanction; 'If you adopt Mr Loutch's plan, you have no occasion of any from me, and until I know the result of this matter I need not be at the pains of making out any unnecessary designs.' A week later he wrote complaining about not being consulted over the new alterations, following it up with another lengthy airing of this and other grievances:

> 'had your Lordship explained your intentions to me about raising the gallery and making your parapets, etc., previous to your leaving this, I could have digested your ideas and given you my opinion in drawings, etc. long since. This you never condescended to do, but have hurried off a man to consult with me about alterations you never seriously spoke of before in my hearing . . . I remember to have spent the best part of a morning in your Lordship's bedchamber a few days before you left this. Our conversation was entirely about the height of the ceiling, but not one word about un-roofing or raising it.'

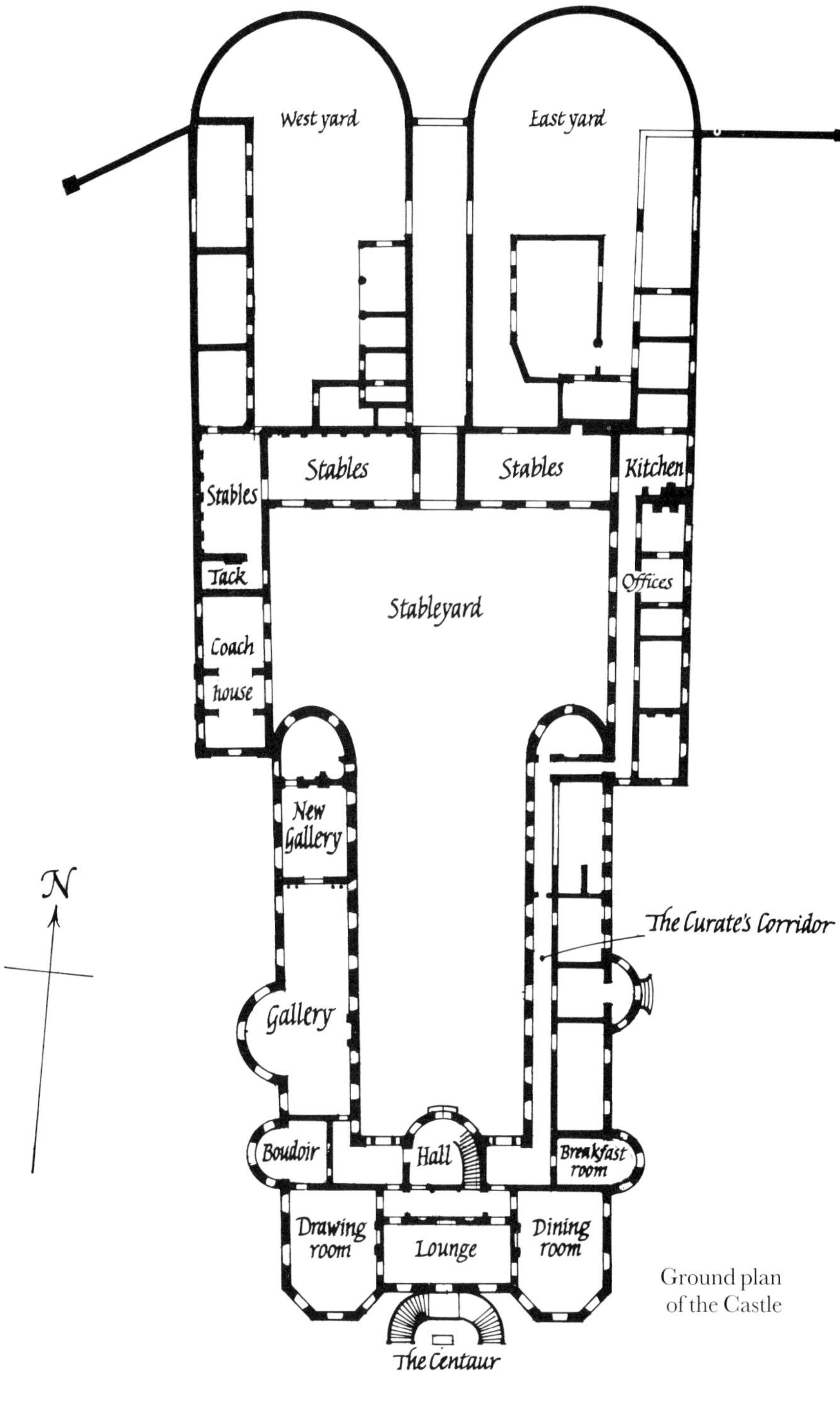

Ground plan
of the Castle

An engraving of the Castle, 1823, by J. P. Neale, with some inaccuracies such as the flat rendering of the south bays.

Meanwhile decorative work was going ahead in the finished parts of the house. The three rooms which faced south received carvings of vine leaves and grapes around doors and window-frames and also an ornamental Wyatt-style entablature. Behind the central lounging room was the grand semicircular staircase covered over with a coffered dome and much expense was lavished on this: scagliola columns, wrought iron balustrades, carved scrollwork and quantities of elaborate stucco work, some of which was done *in situ* and some of which was transported from Dublin. As well as all the extra workmen involved, the joiners, stone-carvers and stuccodores, a German historical painter, Frances Reagal, was also employed to produce decorative panels on ceilings and walls.

The gallery was then again built on to towards the north, to form the library or 'new gallery' with the Bishop's bedchamber above, and finished off with a small dome to match one in a similar position on the east wing. The courtyard plans then began to cause troubles: the McBlains had apparently started a courtyard gateway when they arrived on the site in 1778, but this had to come down again in 1782 and a new one was started in 1783. It seems that Shanahan had had another three-sided row between himself, the Bishop and the

McBlains and had won out with his own design which he described as 'a true Palladian', and which appears to have incorporated a cupola over the stable block which he suggests would be the right place for a clock. The earlier rival designs would have blocked the view of the Temple (see page 39) from the house. John Soane had also produced suggestions for the courtyard and its buildings. Despite all the variations it is difficult to see from the fragments which remain whose ideas emerged as the final ones.

In 1785 a process was started which was to give the whole Castle an appearance of uniformity which at that stage it probably very badly wanted; the McBlains began facing the building with freestone which was quarried from Dungiven and Ballycastle, 'a Surtout of Freestone with the richest Corinthian Pillasters that cd be executed'. Hitherto the Castle must have looked particularly forbidding, being constructed from dark local basalt. While this was going on Shanahan was absent in Cork, and Columbani did the overseeing and

The view of the Temple from the courtyard; the clock is conjectural.

attended to such matters as piping and plumbing for the cisterns and water closets. James McBlain kept the pot boiling by refusing to take orders from Columbani and requiring his instructions to come directly from the Bishop. More rows erupted on Shanahan's return in 1785, upon his finding fault with some carpentry work and with McBlain's 'surtout' casing; no bonding being apparent between the freestone and the stone of the house, and much of the casing being of 'a motley colour, full of various tints of iron ore'. This brought a lengthy and angry rebuttal from David McBlain to the Bishop, defending his work at all points and in particular the maligned bonding: 'He thinks there are not cramps enough in the work. I would be glad to know how any man could tell what quantity of cramps are in a wall from looking at the front of it.'

Shanahan then followed this with another criticism about McBlain's method of carving the fluting on the pilasters before they were erected, insisting that the carving be done when the stones were

A detail from the south front of the Castle showing the McBlain's fine carving of the pilasters.

The castellated seaward-facing side of the Castle, with the false perspective of the buttresses creating the effect of a well defended stronghold.

in position to avoid damage in the course of their installation; he also gets in a stab at Columbani's book-keeping.

Despite all the bickering, the house continued, and from this time onward was evidently fit to be inhabited by the Bishop and his family. At one stage Shanahan makes the rather bizarre suggestion of castellating the entire west side; wisely the Bishop turns the idea down. It is a little unclear when the northernmost castellated 'wings' were added, some sources suggesting 1785 and others not until after the Bishop's death. A later date would support the pleasing notion that when seen from far at sea the 'battlements' would look like a clifftop fortress and thus be a deterrent to any would-be invading French force, a threat taken very seriously in the early 1800s. (Most probably the curved walls were built in 1785, but castellated and buttressed later.) Shanahan seems to have conducted any continuing work *in absentio*, either having to be in England to find suitable slates, or back in Cork to keep an eye on his marble business there – he supplied an impressive selection of chimneypieces to Downhill in July of 1787 – or else deeply involved with the Bishop's next project at Ballyscullion.

When the Bishop died in 1803, the Castle passed into the hands of the man who had taken on the management of his affairs in Ireland, the Rev. Henry Hervey Bruce (see page 146) and subsequently to his heirs. We know very little of the fortunes of the great house other than its escaping serious damage in the 'big wind' of January 1839, until the disastrous fire of May 1851 which destroyed a large part of the interior. The Bishop's fine library was completely destroyed and much of the statuary irretrievably damaged, though it was reported that most of the paintings had been rescued. The then owner of the Castle, Sir Henry Hervey Bruce, suspected that the fire had been

The Bishop's great gallery was turned into a winter garden with the remodelling of the house after the fire of 1851.

started maliciously, and went so far as to issue a notice of £500 reward for information leading to the conviction of a culprit. The restoration of the house was only undertaken between 1870 and 1874 and was supervised by John Lanyon (who was the designer of several Castlerock buildings, including the railway station, and the present house on the Ballyscullion site). Lanyon retained many of the surviving features, though the small domes to the northern wings went, however. He added a new entrance with a small portico to the larger of the two bows of the west front. The cellarage underneath the gallery thus became a hall, which can be seen in the old photographs to have become quickly cluttered up with all the paraphanalia of a late Victorian hunting lodge. The gallery itself was given a new pitch pine ceiling and transformed into a winter garden, stuffed with a formidable array of ferns and potted palms. Lanyon removed the old small pane glazing bars in exchange for large plate glass sash windows; between 1876 and 1877 the Castle was fitted for gas lighting.

The house finally became too much for the Bruce family who had lived there since the Bishop's time until 1922, and it was sold in 1946. During the Second World War it was billeted by servicemen and women of the RAF. By that time some of the contents had been dispersed by auction, a pair of columns going to the library at Bally-

(Above) Lanyon's new entrance hall on the west side of the Castle.
(Right) The new west door, with its pillared portico allied to a curved façade echoing the Bishop's designs at Ballyscullion and Ickworth.

The Castle photographed from the west side in the 1950s. The figures on the cornice are probably workmen engaged in dismantling the roof.

ward in Co. Down, and one of the fine Italian marble chimneypieces ending up at Castle Upton in Co. Antrim. By 1950 the final stage was reached with the removal of the roof and the sale of the surrounding lands, after which the total dissolution of the building became an inevitable process, one which even acquisition by the National Trust in 1980 has failed to check.

Shanahan

MICHAEL SHANAHAN was a native of Cork, so it must be presumed that his association with the Bishop dated from the time when the latter was at Cloyne in 1767. Shanahan had a business in Cork which dealt in marble and cut stone, and which he seems to have been happy to leave to fend for itself for quite long periods, at least if one may so judge from his accompanying the Bishop on his first 'grand tour' in 1770–2. Shanahan's rôle appears to have been as companion to the Bishop's son John Augustus, but more importantly to make drawings of whatever was foremost in the Bishop's interest at the time; just then it was volcanic geology and European bridges. The geology took Shanahan to the middle of France to the Auvergne where, at the Bishop's heels, he found crystalline basalt rock formations very like those of the Giant's Causeway. Shanahan mentions this episode in a letter to the geologist John Strange:

> 'If I thought these sketches which I made of the Giant's Causeway were worth your acceptance I would have sent them long before this. I drew them, to please his Lordship much against my will, knowing it was not in my power to please any person with this kind of work to which I am quite a stranger.' (The Giant's Causeway here being Shanahan's name for the French version.)

Evidently he felt that sketching rock formations was not his true *métier*; perhaps the bridges gave him more satisfaction. Certainly they became a grand project for him, and eventually were engraved and published with the Bishop's help. The Bishop's own interest revolved around his schemes for bridges over the Foyle to Derry and the Bann to Coleraine. The publication of the plates took a long time and was fraught with difficulty; as late as 1786 Shanahan was still pursuing some of the originals: 'I am extremely thankful to your Lordship for the information you were pleased to send me of my drawings. These, with many of my copper-plates which are missing, I have given up for lost many years since.'

Even though the Bishop offered a subscription for 20 copies we do

A selection of some of the churches on which Shanahan may have worked in the diocese of Derry: (top left) Bellaghy, (top right) Church Island, Lough Beg, (below left) Tamlaghtard, and (below right) Tamlaghtfinlagan, Harry Bruce's parish church at Ballykelly.

not know how much of a financial success or otherwise it was for Shanahan. What is clear however is that this early stage in their relationship set a pattern for the years to come, when in all matters to do with building and building management Shanahan was very much the Bishop's right-hand man. Shanahan advised on the addition of a spire to Derry's cathedral and the Foyle bridge scheme even before the great and complicated business of building the Castle. With the building of the Castle, Shanahan's involvement with the Bishop and his affairs reached its greatest. He was architect and planner, works manager, quartermaster, estate manager and accountant all in one. Often these various hats did not fit too well; on his employer complaining about the yield of hay from the estate, he replies indignantly, 'I was not bred a farmer, and yet I have applied myself diligently to it, as I have to every other branch of your Lordship's business . . .' Similarly, after an exchange over the book-keeping for the costs of the Temple he writes:

> '. . . the accounts of the Temple you say are so unsatisfactory that you cannot submit to examine them any more. I am, my Lord, extremely happy to have done with them. I proposed giving them up after Mr. Daniel settled those of the house. Your Lordship then seemed very much dissatisfied; upon which I continued the accounts. And now you are displeased at my manner of keeping them. What mode, my Lord, am I to follow?'

Shanahan's petulance, which in the letters breaks through frequently, is understandable given the breadth of his responsibilities, from the weightiest of matters down to the minutiae – such as supplying writing paper for Lady Erne's bed-chamber – but the tone of much of his correspondence with the Bishop is remarkable, being more like an exchange between social equals than that of an employee and his master. He is capable of the most wilful uncooperativeness, refusing point blank to carry out the designs of another: 'But this much I beg to inform your Lordship, that I am determined (to speak in Cellini's style) never to foster any man's child but one of my own getting. Therefore, if yu. design to put Mr. Loutch's plans into execution, please to order himself or some other person to do it.' While in the same letter he might happily retail to his Lordship some scatalogical workmen's joke in the poorest of taste. Mrs Anne

Dunboe Glebe house, designed by Shanahan. Originally the front door had been built on the other (north) side of the house.

Shanahan, who assisted with the housekeeping at the Castle, could also be free with complaints for her Bishop, especially when he brought company without giving her enough prior notice to stock up: 'this whole Country will hardly produce things good enough, at least as good as your Lordship would wish, to entertain . . . with.'

Whatever the master/servant relationship, Shanahan stayed with the Bishop for many years and, perhaps more remarkably, completed many of his building projects. In addition to the Castle, he was responsible for the Temple, The Mausoleum, probably for the Lion and Bishop's Gates, Drumagully Bridge and, of course, for Ballyscullion. He may also have been the architect for many of the Bishop's church and spire building projects: Tamlaghtfinlagan, Tyanee, Banagher and possibly Belaghy. He was also responsible for Dunboe Glebe House which was built in 1774, and which in the 1820s became the home of Archdeacon Monsell (father of the celebrated writer of hymns). And while all this work was going on in the North, Shanahan had also to think about projects in his home county and his marble working business there. He was said to have built the first St Patrick's Bridge for the city of Cork, and it would seem that a letter from him to the Bishop, dated 1787, concerned the preparatory engineering work for this: '. . . this instance is the most interesting part of my undertaking. I have just finished a cofferdam at the expense of £600. My pumps will be ready by monday next for draining the dams. The attention and the eyes of the public are now watching my operations'. Cork also had to thank him for its City & County Jail, among other 'public works'.

Nor was he backward about promoting the marble works (which in 1786 employed no less than 28 men) as may be deduced from a memo to the Bishop disparaging his imported chimney pieces: 'In your Lordship's bed-chamber the mantle of the chimneypiece is bent down in the middle and endangers the falling of the frieze and tablet. This is one of your English chimneypieces . . . I took the dimensions of them to get new ones made.' Little imagination is required to guess where the new ones were going to be made! The marble works in Cork also supplied such items as the leopards for the Lion Gate and the Earl-Bishop's arms over the door of the Temple.

Shanahan appears from all the evidence to have been very much a man of parts, ready and able to turn his hand and his considerable business skills to many different things. His business acumen would be well proven, even without any other witness, by the fact of his managing to cope with the Bishop as employer for over 20 years.

The Bishop's arms over the door of the Temple.

Sir John Soane

JOHN SOANE only finds a place in the Downhill story because of what-might-have-been. It seems most likely that as a young man, studying in Rome on a scholarship from the Royal Academy, he met the Bishop some time in the latter part of 1778. The Bishop was evidently much taken with the young architect and presented him with copies of Palladio and Vitruvius – sacred texts for all eighteenth-century architects – from his own library. In December of 1778 the Bishop was heading for Naples where the milder winter weather and company of his old friend Sir William Hamilton would doubtless speed his recovery from a recent illness: with him went Soane, and en route the two indulged in much architectural archaeology. They were particularly pleased with the ancient site of the Villa of Lucullus, where they had a picnic. Soane measured and sketched and it is possible that with hints from the Bishop, the episode gave rise to a design for a dining room for Downhill based on the celebrated Roman gourmet's own palace. While still in Rome Soane had sketched out large additions for the existing south-facing front of the Castle, and it looks very much from the surviving drawings that it was the intention to make one of these 'pavilions' house the Roman feasting room. It may also have been this pavilion design which had so irritated Shanahan (see page 12), who was having to deal with the real construction work as well as the Bishop's sudden whims.

On arrival in Naples after Christmas more schemes were proposed such as a mausoleum to contain the commemorative statue of the Bishop's brother (see page 128), commissioned from van Nost to stand in the grounds of Downhill. Soane probably already had a design for such a Mausoleum, based loosely on the Roman model at St-Rémy, France. Another idea was for a dog kennel, again on classic lines, though in this case no model from the antique existed; Soane rose to the occasion and produced a remarkable design, tripartite with concave sides and a shallow central dome, and with suitable canine decoration where required. Had the Bishop's patronage of Soane not failed and this extraordinary *turgurium* for the hounds of

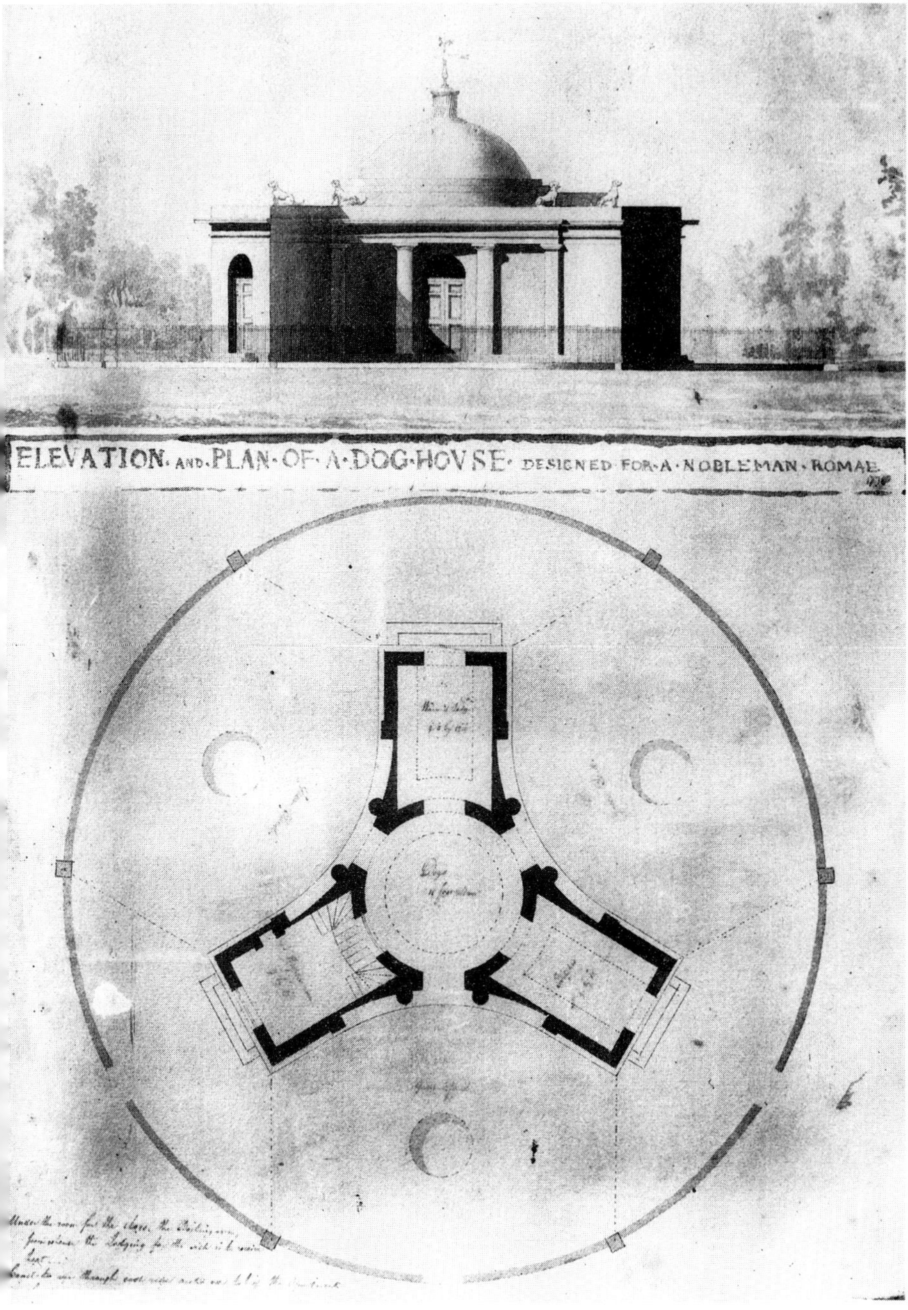

Soane's design for a dog kennel for Downhill, drawn in Italy but never built.

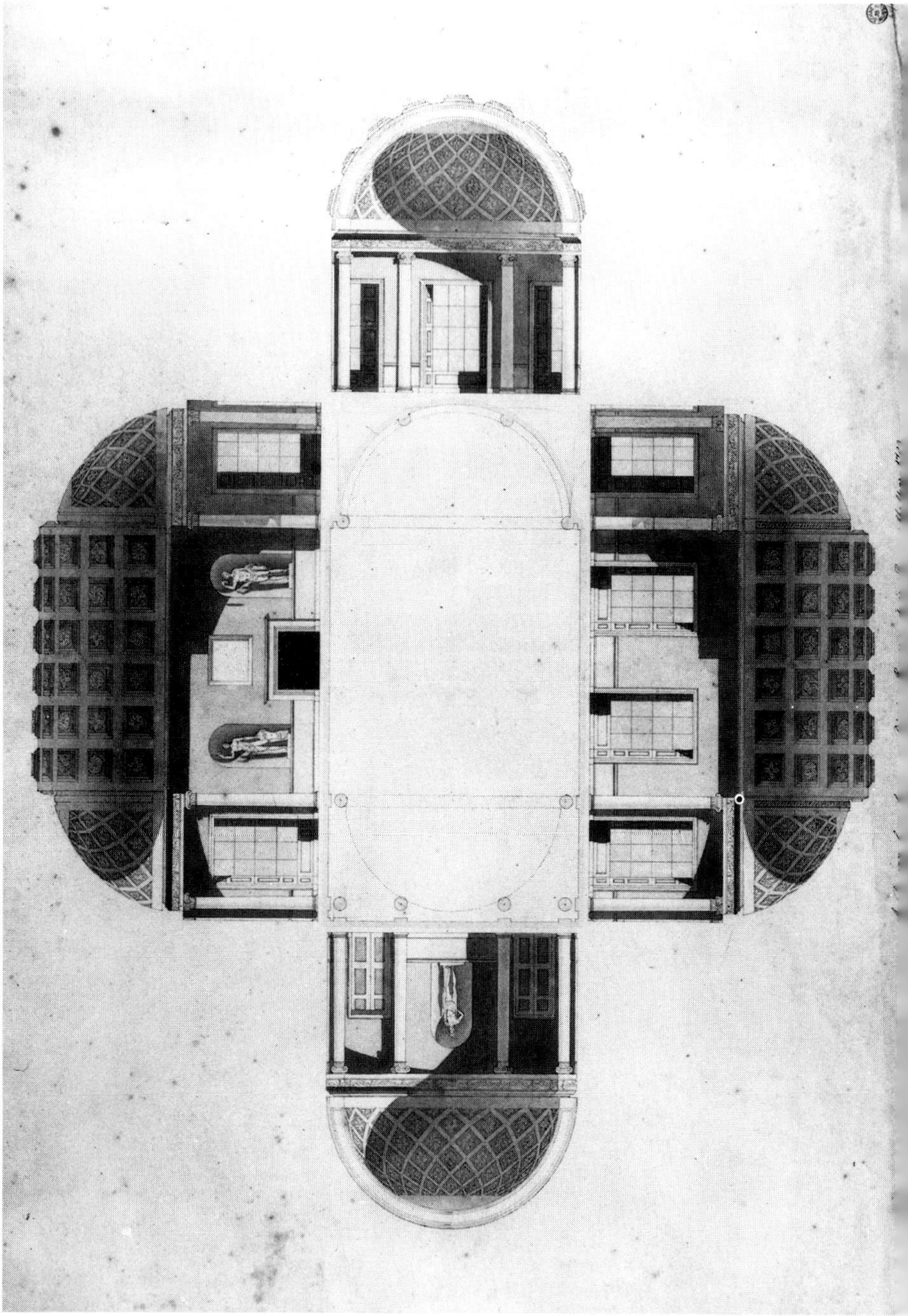

Soane's design for a 'Summer Dining Room' for Downhill, drawn in Rome in 1780 and although favoured by the Bishop never built.

his eldest son been built, what a remarkable addition to the Downhill skyline it would have been.

Yet another notion was a re-creation at Downhill of the famous Temple of Vesta at Tivoli, of which Soane had been requested to make accurate drawings. Again the young architect's involvement with the project stopped at that point.

In 1780 at the end of July, Soane travelled to Ireland and stayed at Downhill for about five weeks. He tried to make sense of the work which had been done there already with a view to somehow incorporating the plans he had proposed for the buildings while with the Bishop in Italy, namely the two schemes for dining rooms contained in the 'pavilions'. However, the state of affairs on the site together with the antagonism which we may safely assume to have emanated from the exasperated Shanahan must have made matters very difficult for him. It seems that the courtyard at the back or northern side of the house was being built in the most haphazard way but at the same time was being considered as the main entrance approach. Soane discussed with the Bishop, drew sketches and argued his case. At one stage there was a proposal to make a colonnaded corridor to shelter the approach from the stables to the north. The contentious 'pavilions' were dropped. The Bishop wanted a 'new room' (possibly the genesis of the picture gallery) on the west side of the courtyard; Soane tried to salvage one of his eating-room designs – they having been jettisoned with the pavilions – to serve the changed situation. At one moment Soane appeared to have got the whole sorry mess into some kind of control: he had been to the quarries in Ballycastle to make a deal over the supply of top quality freestone, he had managed to procure the services of reliable carpenters form Armagh, and he had found a way, as he thought, of pinning the Bishop down to given procedures by presenting itemised lists of requirements. Methodically he set about putting right some of the existing defects: smoking chimneys; floors and ceilings without soundproofing; doors, windows and shutters which did not fit; and above all no water closets or water supply.

After many more conferences, agreement appeared to have been reached over the new 'gallery' and even some compromise reached over the appearance of the south entrance front, but then, suddenly, as he noted in his diary, 'Monday. Everything entirely changed'. At this point he packed his bags and left, and afterwards claimed that he had only been reimbursed with £30 for all his work and his expenses.

Soane went on to become one of the most original architects of his age. Most of his work on the Bank of England no longer survives but London's Dulwich Picture Gallery and his own remarkable house in Lincoln's Inn Fields testify to his genius. Of his work at Downhill all that was carried out were the alterations to Lady Erne's bedchamber and the installation of a water system.

The Mausoleum

WHEN GEORGE, the 2nd Earl of Bristol and elder brother to the Bishop, died in March of 1775, he was deeply mourned. Writing to his friend, Strange, only a week after, the Bishop says:

> 'Within the last few days I have lost the kindest and the most affectionate brother. This has blunted in me every sense of pleasure, and left me a mass and lump of inanimate matter. He has testified his kindness to me to the last; but no accession of wealth, especially to one in my situation, can compensate for the loss of a real friend . . .'

The 'kindness' the Bishop refers to was threefold. In the first place his brother had procured his position for him; although George only held his position of Lord Lieutenant of Ireland for a year before resigning it in 1767, he lost no time in having his younger brother preferred first for the Bishopric of Cloyne and subsequently for Derry – then the richest living in the island – and secondly he left the Bishop the considerable sum of £10,000 in his will. The third, but less foreseeable, advantage was that George's death put the Bishop in the running for the Bristol title, something which as the youngest son he could never have expected. In fact he had only to wait four years before the middle brother Augustus also died leaving no legitimate children.

So it is not very surprising that the Bishop felt it appropriate to erect a grandiose monument to the elder brother who had literally made his fortune. The idea of having a mausoleum placed at a point of vantage in the demesne as an eye-catcher or ornament to the landscape was a popular one in this, the age of the picturesque. Thus, the Bishop may well have had a good idea of what he wanted before he commissioned the famous Dublin based sculptor, van Nost, to produce a full length life-size statue of George, in 1778. Elizabeth, the Bishop's second daughter who was married to John Foster and was living in Dunleer Co. Louth, was instructed to keep an eye on the sculptor; the Bishop wrote, 'I have bespoke a full-length

LUDERE QUÆ VELLEM
SEX·L·M·IVLIEI·C·F·PARENTIBVS·SVEIS
Feet
Metres

A reconstruction of the Downhill Mausoleum (far left) compared with the Roman original at St-Rémy. (Right) Soane's sketch for a mausoleum on broadly similar lines.

statue of my late brother wch I mean to have executed by the print we have of him, and beg that you & your husband would visit the work as often as you can.'

The model for the mausoleum in which this sculpture was to be placed was that of the Roman tomb at St-Rémy in Provence, an ancient monument much admired by antiquarians and architects of the time. Indeed, when the Bishop was in Rome in 1778 and met the young English architect John Soane he very likely would have seen

A watercolour view of Downhill painted by John Nixon *c.*1810, showing the Mausoleum to the left of the house, the glen in the foreground and little evidence of tree planting.

Soane's design for a 'sepuchral monument' – he may even have commissioned it – which follows the St-Rémy model formally, if not literally. In the event the building of the mausoleum went ahead according to the design of Michael Shanahan and, unlike the Castle and the Temple, it seems not to have been the subject of many changes of mind. In about 1779 Shanahan submitted an estimate of cost for the structure and made the rather curious suggestion that it might incorporate an ice-house: 'I am sorry to find, my Lord, this estimate exceed your expectations, but considered the magnificence and elegance of the Mausoleum I do not think it dear. That at St-Rémy is but 50 feet high, and I believe would cost about £340. The ice-house, if built under it, will cost £13. 15s.'

In fact the estimate, at £426 9s., seems comparatively modest. The proposed ice-house (see page 54) was built later, in 1786, under the supervision of David McBlain, and in a more appropriate position to the west of the demesne. As built, the Mausoleum differs from the St-Rémy one, being both larger originally and somewhat simpler in its decoration. Today we see only the plinth, the Palladian style pavilion with its ionic columns and pilasters, and above that the circular drum which would have supported eight corinthian columns in turn supporting a dome (as in the Soane drawing) or a cone (as at St-Rémy). The Lord Lieutenant's statue stood originally within the corinthian columns, although at one stage Shanahan had tried to persuade his patron that the sculpture would look as well if mounted in the lower part: 'Mausoleum: as I have now plenty of timber for my scaffolding, whether will your Lordship have the figure erected between the Ionic columns or the Corinthian? It would look well between the former, and save great trouble.' That was written in May of 1783, and although it suggests that the work was under way, Shanahan was still drawing plans in November of the same year; he writes 'On receipt of your Lordship's letter, I began to draw a fair plan of the mausoleum, which I hope to finish tomorrow and send off on thursday morning. The original plan I have by me is all soiled and not fit to send.' Probably the dirtied copy was the one which was being used by the masons. Shanahan was pleased with the Mausoleum as it came to be built and thought that it was better than the Roman one. The inscription which runs around the entablature is from the classic poet Virgil, and reads:

> 'Ille meas Errare Boves ut cernis, et ipsum
> Ludere quae Vellum Calamo permisit agresti.'

This would translate, approximately, as: 'He permitted my oxen to wander, as you see, and allowed me to play on the rustic pipe whatever I wished.' – a somewhat curious dedication of thanks from a bishop.

Unfortunately, the north Derry coastline proved not to be the Arcady of the poet, and in 1839 the monument was severely damaged in a violent storm, 'The Big Wind'. The cupola and its supporting ring of eight corinthian columns were blown down and with it the statue of George. This disaster inspired one William Boyce to publish some verses in the style of McGonagall on the subject in 1843:

'Terrific howled the Hurricane around,
And laid the marble statue o'er the ground;
Charta, columns, marbles, pedestal and base,
Fair superstructure once, but ruined now!'

Today much of the 'fair superstructure' still lies about the base of the Mausoleum, but the body of van Nost's celebrated statue has been rescued and placed behind the Bishop's Gate; his head has never been recovered, although among the 'Downhill Marbles' (see page xx) is a hopelessly weathered head which would certainly have been a strong contender. It is a sad, but not totally inappropriate fate for an English nobleman who held the title of Lord Lieutenant for only one year, and in fact never set foot in Ireland.

A fragment of the upper part of the Mausoleum, blown down in the gale of 1839.

The Mussenden Temple

THE MUSSENDEN TEMPLE is perhaps the finest surviving piece of all the Bishop's architectural ventures in Ireland; whatever else, it is complete.

The idea of the Temple may have been in the Bishop's head for some time before he gave instructions for its building in 1783. At one time the Bishop had toyed with the idea of buying and removing the Temple of Vesta at Tivoli – stone by stone one must assume – to Ireland; but the Roman authorities objected to an act of plunder which would only have been equalled by that of the Elgin Marbles, and so he decided to build his own version. The design of the Temple was based loosely on that of Bramante for the temple on Monte Gianicolo in Rome, but as usual the working designs were drawn up by Michael Shanahan. For once the work seemed to go forward without too many hiccups and although James McBlain is recorded as having carved one capital in the Ionic style before the Bishop changed his mind in favour of the Corinthian order, the whole building was completed in just two years. The Bishop had the Temple constructed in honour of his cousin and good friend Mrs Mussenden (see page 46).

Originally it was intended to have been of bare basalt construction, this stone being available locally, and having already been used in the construction of the Castle. However, in the event the Temple was built of brick, Bann brick (see page 45) on a base of basalt, and with the whole exterior clad in freestone facing, this stone having to be brought by boat all the way round the coast from Ballycastle. The McBlains, father and son, carved all the external ornamentation, the '4 mitres . . . 4 Leapords . . . 4 coronets in Frise', except for the Bishop's arms which appear over the entrance; this was cut in Portland stone in Shanahan's marble works in Cork, and not installed until 1788.

The Temple's domed roof went through some construction variations before being finally covered in 'Slate in the pattin Stile'. Shanahan had initially hoped that the Bishop would let him cover it with gilded metal, it 'would make a glorious figure' he wrote, but then went on to compromise with copper or lead. (Today the dome is covered with copper.) At one stage Shanahan also suggested a glazed light for the dome: 'What would your Lordship think of making a circular window in the top of the Dome of 6 feet Diameter? This would finely enlighten all the upper part of the inside' he wrote in 1783. This may even have been carried out, if a letter of David McBlain is to be credited ('Finished Temple Skylight'), but then was changed again later. Whatever happened, the Temple eventually received a beautifully proportioned dome surmounted by a conventional carved urn. The skylight in the dome idea was later carried out at Ballyscullion. The Bishop chose a quotation from the classical author Lucretius to be cut in the frieze all around the outside:

> 'Suave mari magno, turbantibus aequora ventis,
> E terra alterius magnum spectare laborem.'

In Dryden's loose translation: 'Tis pleasant, safely to behold from shore/The tossing ship, and hear the tempest roar.' Today it is rather difficult to read the whole inscription in safety because we can no longer walk right round the Temple as might have been possible when it was built. Curiously, the word order of the inscription is not quite the same as that of the original, 'magnum' and 'alterius' being transposed on the Temple. Could the Bishop, a fluent linguist and dilettante of classical scholarship, have possibly got the quotation wrong? Or perhaps his workmen who were not versed in the great Latin authors made the mistake. Originally the inscription was made from gilded metal letters – like the 'Brilliant Metal' that Shanahan had wanted to use for the dome – and it was thought that the verse was continued on the inside (Non quia vexari quemquam'st jucunda voluptas/sed, quibus ipse malis careas, quia cernere suave'st 'Not because it is a pleasure that anyone should be troubled, but because it is a pleasure to see what misfortune you lack').

The interior of the Temple was designed to house part of the Bishop's library, but would almost certainly have contained some art treasures as well; possibly classical or neo-classical busts would have adorned the circular alcoves above the window level. The bookcases would have been placed between interior pilasters and these may have originally been finished with *scagliola* a plaster coating which imitates marble or porphyry. Together with the coloured plasterwork of the interior of the dome, it must have all looked very rich

The Temple of Vesta at Tivoli, the inspiration for the Bishop's own clifftop temple.

and splendid. Some local Downhill anecdotes concern the inside decorations: one story has it that the art of plastering was so jealously guarded by the artisans that the Temple door was kept locked while the work was in progress and their materials were passed in to them secretly – another tale, perhaps connected to the first, was that they dispensed with the encumbrance of clothes while working so as not to ruin them with plaster. It is not known exactly how the inside looked during the Bishop's time, but occasionally little plaster rosettes have been found and they may well have been part of the ceiling which was evidently coffered in blue and gilt.

The Bishop loved books. Moreover, he loved books for their contents rather than as the decorative objects that some of his contemporaries took them for. In *c.*1789 he wrote to his daughter Mary describing the library of a certain Count MacCarthy in Toulouse which he termed 'the very greatest curiosity of All Europe in its way'. Here were books so highly decorated and exquisitely bound that they were 'not intended to be read but to be admir'd'. Such books as the Bishop had installed in the Temple would have to be cared for and since one of the greatest enemies of books is damp that meant that the Temple must have a heating system. Originally it must have been some kind of fireplace because in 1783 we find Shanahan writing to his patron about the placing of the chimneypiece *in the window* opposite the door, and even having doubts of his own about what seems to be a most extraordinary infelicity of design: 'it will disfigure the window in which it is placed, and the funnel can never be cleaned.' It is difficult to see where, in the main part of the Temple, Shanahan might have placed the grate which he had purchased in London in 1789 specially for the purpose, but the final solution to the problem was to build the fireplace in the 'crypt'. It is in the seaward side of the structure with the flue rising to roof level within the wall.

The library had also to be dusted, and this job was still being carried out some 11 years after the Bishop had left Ireland for the last time, as we know from the contents of a rather pathetic letter from one Arthur McMacklin whose task it was; he stated that he was 83 years old, was recently widowed and had never been paid any wages, but also hoped that he might be allowed to continue as he was 'still capable of taking the proper care of the books in the Temple'.

The building of the Temple was carefully accounted, and we form quite a vivid picture of the Bishop's business acumen in his inspection of the account books; evidently the Bishop became dissatisfied with the book-keeping methods of Robert McGhee, the rector of Desertmartin, who signed off his checking of the figures with an ambivalent phrase which stated that they were correct as far as he could see but that there might still be errors! After this the Bishop took over the matter himself and did his own adding up, describing McGhee as an 'ingrained and thorough-paced sinner'. The cost of the building came to something slightly in excess of £1,169 7s. 3d., a total recorded when it was practically complete. This would represent a huge amount of money today, and it is certainly rather more than Shanahan's original estimate of £426.

The history of the Temple after its completion has not been without incident. It has been thought that prior to the United Irishmen rising of 1798 the Temple was used for the planning of that event, and although its isolated position and all-round views would have made it quite a good place for a clandestine meeting, the idea does seem rather unlikely; certainly the Bishop – or his steward – would not have countenanced such a use at that time, when his own politics were becoming anti-revolutionary, most especially with regard to

The Mussenden Temple

Downhill engraved by J. P. Neale, from *Views of the Seats of Noblemen and Gentlemen*, 1821. Although suspect in some details – the Mausoleum seems to be drawn as an obelisk – it clearly shows the Temple at some distance from the edge of the cliff

the French, 'that Nation of Baboons'. It is hard to imagine that, despite his earlier enthusiasms for a more democratically governed Ireland, he would have approved a French landing at Killala by those 'damned Blackguard, pilfering, plundering, pillaging Republicans.'

However reactionary the Bishop may have become in his later years, which were spent on the continent of Europe, his ecumenical attitude towards the Catholics in Derry did not change. He permitted the 'crypt' of the Temple to be used for the celebration of Mass and went further in allocating £10 per annum for the officiating priest as well as providing his Sunday breakfast and a feed for his horse. This generosity was continued by the Bishop's inheritor, the Rev. Henry Hervey Bruce (see page 142). Worship in the Temple is one of the tangible links we have with the Bishop today, in that since 1981 a dawn service has been held there on Easter Sundays.

The Temple was inherited by the Bruce family along with the Bishop's other Irish possessions and remained as part of the estate until being acquired by a Mr F. W. Smyth after the last war. The

National Trust of Northern Ireland accepted the Temple as a gift from Mr Smyth in 1949 and began a programme of restoration which included replacing the fabric of the roof. Unfortunately, at the end of 1952 a severe winter gale took most of the new copper off the dome, setting both the work and the budget back considerably. Today the Temple receives many thousands of visitors every year and has even been used for concerts of music; in June 1986 the *Lyrica Musica* String Quartet and the Ulster College of Music performed there a programme of chamber works and madrigals; since then the Temple has been used regularly once a year for music recitals and poetry reading. In glorious weather in June 1995 the Temple was the setting for a one-man play, 'The Earl-Bishop', with Denys Hawthorne in the title rôle. The piece which was specially commissioned from local playwright Harry Barton by the National Trust North Coast Member's Association was such a success that an extra performance had to be staged by popular demand. We can be sure that both the Bishop and Mrs Mussenden would have been totally delighted.

Bann bricks

'Bann bricks', which were used in many of the buildings of the area, were made at various locations along the river Bann from about 1750 onwards: at Eden on the Antrim side, at Drumail on the Derry side and also at Agivy Bridge. Each worker had their own clay pit and children were employed to form the bricks at the staggering rate of 1100 per day; it being assumed that this total allowed for the 'failure' of 100 bricks. Bricks were laid out on the grass to dry before being sent to communal kilns for firing.

A detail from the Temple; this motif is called a *Vitruvian scroll* or 'running dog' and can also be seen on the cornice of the Castle.

Mrs Mussenden

MRS MUSSENDEN was born Frideswide Bruce – the strange Christian name is taken from that of the patron saint of Oxford. Her father was descended from a Scottish branch of the Bruces and her mother was the daughter of the Bishop's uncle, Henry Hervey-Aston. She married in 1781 one Daniel Mussenden, a wealthy banker, and met the Bishop just a year later when he came to stay with them in their home at Larchfield, Co. Down.

By all accounts the Bishop was captivated by this very pretty young woman, and indeed she was most attractive, as we may judge both from her portrait and from the accounts of contemporaries. The Bishop had only recently quarrelled with his long-suffering wife and had left her at Ickworth, so one can perhaps imagine the delight he took in the company of his 'chère cousine' whose 'dear innocent countenance is sufficient to animate and enliven all around her' as he put it in a letter of that time. He loved to hear her perform on the harpsichord, and on occasions when she paid a visit to Downhill was recorded in joining in with one of the Bishop's favourite amusements at table, that of proposing humorous toasts. They were evidently very good friends.

Unfortunately the world was not to see the relationship as being the innocent thing that now, with hindsight, it is generally supposed to have been. In the late eighteenth century a lady's honour was more easily compromised, and if the lady was beautiful, married and only in her twenties, and if the man was 30 years her senior, also married and a prelate to boot, it is hardly surprising that a scandal of sorts ensued. The Bishop had plenty of enemies, and one of them published a letter in the *Freeman's Journal* of 1783 more or less accusing the Bishop of being more to Mrs Mussenden than was consistent with his rôle of a 'Bon papa'. The names were not spelt out, but it was obvious who was intended; the writer hid under the pen-name 'Scaevola' (the allusion is rather obscure, Mucius Scaevola being the ancient Roman who burnt his own hand to punish it for assassinating the wrong man). A reply, vindicating the Bishop, was published in the *Volunteer Evening Post*, and signed 'An Inhabitant of Lisburne'.

Mrs Mussenden, from a miniature

We also know that the Bishop thought of bringing an action against the *Freeman*, but in the event decided not to go through with it, probably very wisely.

Mrs Mussenden died very young in 1785; thus the Temple which the Bishop had started to build in her honour during her lifetime was to become her memorial (see page 39). It seems unlikely that the 'scandal' could have had anything to do with her early death, but it is just possible that the Bishop felt an indirect responsibilty, and might go a little way to explaining why he eventually left all his Irish property to her brother, the Rev. Henry Hervey Bruce, and not to his own sons (see page 142).

The Lion Gate

THE LION GATE as it is now called was apparently the first entrance to the Castle. It may be assumed that it was under construction in 1783, as indicated by a letter from Shanahan to his patron: 'West gate to the demesne: a small door in either wall joining the piers would be very useful.' Whether the doors mentioned were originally sanctioned is not clear, though old photographs certainly show that there was a door in the westward wall in the late nineteenth century. As with the initial plan for the Castle, the gates loosely follow designs by Wyatt, and would have had little porter's lodges on either side of each curved curtain wall. Although one lodge was still to be seen in a picture of *c.*1880, they have now both disappeared.

The Lion Gate was so called because of the two figures which originally crowned either pier, but in fact this is a misnomer – the correct heraldic name for these beasts was 'ounce', an old name for the snow leopard. Shanahan was thus rather more accurate in referring to them as 'Leopards' when he wrote in a letter in a letter of 1787: 'I have lately sustained a very great loss by the death of a most excellent carver, otherwise I would have sent the leopards for the demesne gate.' It seems that Shanahan had the 'leopards' made at his workshop in Cork, and had them transported from one end of the country to the other (as he did with other architectural decorations for Downhill). Both the ounces were still standing on their respective piers at the turn of the century, but today there is only one; his partner, greatly worn by the effects of the weather, was placed in the crypt of the Temple in 1964, where it stayed until 1992 when it was moved to a more public position in front of the Bishop's Gate Lodge.

It is not quite certain who carved the figures, or indeed who was the carver Shanahan lost, but payment for a 'leopord' in the year 1787 is credited to a Thomas McWilliams, and another in 1780 to a Mr Foy concerning the same. It has also been suggested that they were made locally by a Mr McCullough (whose son became a famous actor in the nineteenth century).

(Above) a late nineteenth century pencil sketch of the Lion Gate showing part of the lodge. Note the surveyor's triangulation mark on the base of the left pier. (Left) the same pier with its remaining 'ounce'.

The Bishop's Gate

PROPERLY SPEAKING the 'Bishop's' Gate is also a misnomer; originally it was known as the Coleraine Gate or the Coleraine Battalion Arch. It was built between 1783 and 1784 and was intended to commemorate the Coleraine Battalion of the Volunteers as well as providing a 'picturesque' main entrance to the estate. It is 'picturesque' because this approach to the Castle allows it first to be seen from the distance and then hides it as the avenue advances through the glen, only to reveal it again from a different angle: 'losing the object, to draw nigh obliquely'. It is reasonably certain that the Gate was finished in 1784, as Shanahan received payments in July of that year for his supervising, and probably the design, of the work. The carving and stone cutting was done by James McBlain. The Bishop gave a large dinner for the officers of

The Bishop's Gate and gate lodge

the Coleraine Battalion in the same year, so it is likely that the Gate was completed for that event. The hospitality offered to the officers was so extensive that the final bill came to £37. 5s. 1d. (Mrs Shanahan had to go to great lengths to buy enough provisions, not to mention mugs and extra blankets, for the guests.)

The arch and its flanking walls are very elegantly designed and bear the influence of James Wyatt. The frieze of the gate has alternate mitres and ox-skulls carved in relief; it has been thought that the skulls were a reference to the cow of Dunboe (see page 179) but unfortunately for this theory they were a fairly common decorative device – properly called 'bucrania' – in classic and neo-classic architecture. Similar skulls appeared on the interior decoration of the Castle, as witnessed by plaster versions once collected in the crypt of

the Temple, but now together with the other 'Downhill Marbles'. The Bishop's crest with the 'ounce' appears in a plaque surmounted by his earl's coronet on the front of the pediment, while on the *back* of the pediment it is surmounted by his Bishop's mitre. The sculpted figure of Diana the Huntress which stands in the left-hand niche was probably originally part of the Bishop's collection; in old photographs of the inside of the Castle she appears to have stood in a niche in the hall staircase landing.

The Bishop's episcopal arms from the back of the Bishop's Gate (top). The statue of Diana (above) on the main staircase landing in the Castle at the end of the nineteenth century.

The Gate Lodge

Although the Gate Lodge appears to be different in design to the Gate itself, it was probably built shortly after it was completed. This may be inferred from a note written by the Bishop's Italian architect Columbani in 1784, 'the Stone, Lime and sand I have seen at the Coleraine Gate – is sufficient to build the Lodge to the height, pointed out by Mr James McBlain.' The design and building of the Lodge is thought to be by James McBlain, partly because of its resemblance to work he did earlier at Hillsborough Church. The 'Gothick' style in which the lodge was built might not, at first, seem to be quite in the Bishop's character, good classicist as we know him to have been; but this would be to forget that in Ireland at least the 'correct' architectural mode for the established church still paid lip-service to the gothic – the Bishop was, after all, very fond of that very gothic feature, the spire – and also that this style was more or less the 'latest thing'. The wiggly design of the window and door surrounds is called 'vermiculation', so called because of its worm-like appearance.

McBlain's monument in Old Dunboe churchyard.

The Dovecote & ice-house

As with the fishponds (see page 56), the dovecote and ice-house fulfilled a dual purpose in both supplying the Bishop's table and in providing a picturesque addition to the demesne. It was added to the end of the walled garden in about 1786 and was built by David McBlain. The circular form was typical for a dovecote but no doubt McBlain gave the roof a dome shape similar to that of the Temple so as to create a related silhouette for the skyline when viewed from the western windows of the Castle. In place of the Temple's urn, the dovecote has a small octagonal structure which served as a ventilator. A set of openings on the southern side of the building permitted

The dovecote seen from the walled garden, choked with ivy and strewn with rubble, as it was before the National Trust acquired the property and restored it after 1987.

the birds to fly in and out, and on the inside the walls are lined with niches for them to nest in. Originally there would also have been a 'potence', or central pole with side arms, which would have revolved to provide a resting place for a ladder so that each nesting niche at every level was accessible.

Below the dovecote was the ice-house. In the winter months ice would be gathered from the depression in the field to the north of the building and then packed into the ice-house, probably with insulation in the form of sawdust or shavings. The ice-house was used in much the same way as the modern refrigerator to store perishable food so that it might be enjoyed out of season; the idea was by no means a new one even in the time of the Bishop, the first ice-house having been built for Charles II in St James's Park in 1660. It is pleasing to think that the Bishop might have easily enjoyed ice-cream when in residence at Downhill; it would certainly have been available in France and Italy in the late eighteenth century, so he might well have had a taste for it.

Dungannon Hill

In the West Glen there is a large circular mound which in ancient times was a fort, or dun, whose history may date back to the time of the chieftain of the area. In 1182 a great battle took place here, resulting in the defeat of Donnell O'Loughlin by the Normans.

In 1783 the Bishop had the top levelled off, an operation which required the use of gunpowder for 'blowing stones' and the whole mound planted with trees. Before that time it had been known as 'The Giant's Grave' but in its improved state it was to be known as 'Dungannon Hill' in honour of the Volunteer Convention at Dungannon in 1782 and 1783 in which the Bishop had taken such a great interest (see page 97).

Lady Erne's Seat

This curious structure, overlooking Portvantage, is sometimes described as a folly and sometimes as a gazebo. The style of its building is identical to the castellated wings which were added to the stable block of the Castle after the Bishop's time. It is probable therefore that it is *not* the 'Lady Erne's Seat' mentioned in workmen's accounts

Lady Erne's seat

of the year 1783. In August of that year Shanahan wrote '... I enclose your Lordship's estimates of the grotto...' and earlier, a bill of 'Jenry ye 18 1783' relates 'Due to John Heaslet for cutting out a seat in the Glen in portvanteg. £0. 10. 0.' This document is endorsed on the back by the Bishop: 'Lady Erne's Seat in Portvantage'. Mr Heaslet was also employed 'blasting stons' – in other words landscaping – in Portvantage Glen. That which is *now* known as Lady Erne's Seat was probably put up by the Bishop's successor Harry Bruce, and though suggestions as to its use range from a tea-house to a hide for wild-fowlers, or even as a winnowing floor, it was most likely first thought of as an eye-catcher to make a romantic silhouette when viewed from the castle. Where the grotto cut out by Mr Heaslet really was is a matter for conjecture, though on one of the lower paths below the folly there is indeed a kind of niche in the rock overlooking the Portvantage Glen and in an excellent position to catch the morning sun. Perhaps we shall never know for certain.

The Fishponds

The Downhill demesne boasted two fishponds in the Bishop's day. The first to be created was in the Portvantage Glen where, by damming the flow of water from the glen at the seaward end, an artificial lake was formed. The other long fishpond which we know was created in 1787 is in the West Glen; excavation was required for this lake and again it had to be dammed at its northern end by Drumagully Bridge (see map page 164). The ponds were stocked through the help of Lord Moira who, in 1797, wrote to say that although all the stock fish from one of his estates in Co. Down had apparently been stolen, he would be happy to supply fish from his palace at Montalto, near Ballynahinch: 'I speak now of Carp particularly, as I am uncertain whether the tench have (bred) or not. I have a pond full of gudgeons which breed amazingly & I think are little inferior to Smelts.' He continued in the letter to say that the fishes could be transported to Downhill in 'one of the great Bottles that the Bleachers use to hold oil of Vitriol.' It is to be hoped that the bottle was well washed out first!

When the National Trust acquired the Portvantage Glen in 1960, the fishpond was completely clogged with reeds and used to dry out in fine weather. The pond was reclaimed and a new dam built through an unemployment relief scheme in about 1968 (the West Glen was taken over by the Department of Forestry). The idea of having fresh fish handy for the table was a lot older than the eighteenth century, having been developed in the middle ages, especially in monastic communities whose rules included days when meat might not be eaten. Having two large ponds may seem excessive nowadays, but then they would also have been regarded as decorative picturesque 'improvements' to the landscape.

Although today neither pond is stocked with carp any more, they are frequented by varieties of waterfowl, including dabchicks, mallard and moorhens.

Moorhen

Ballyscullion

BALLYSCULLION is little more than a memory today. The Bishop's second great house was begun in 1787 on the west side of Lough Beg, which placed it on the very edge of the see of Derry. The Bishop was extremely astute in the business of managing and acquiring land, if not always entirely scrupulous. He had obtained the lands along the shore of the lough when, in a letter to his eldest daughter Mary, he wrote that the 'Leasehold estate of Ld Massareene wch fell into me' and the building of the new 'folly', as contemporaries were to call it, began in the same year. It is significant to note that, at the time of the acquisition, Lord Massareene was in prison in France.

What was it that induced in Bishop to start another great 'edifying' venture? He had the old house at Ickworth in Suffolk, the 'Casino' in Derry (see page 11) and of course Downhill, which although complete and being occupied was still constantly being added to and generally tinkered with. It is difficult to say, but we must always remember that the Bishop was a truly protean character, one whose mind was never fixed steadfastly on one subject for any great length of time, and also that one of the passions to which he returned regularly throughout his life was the love of art. Bearing this in mind it is quite possible that, having created in Downhill a house set in the rugged grandeur which would have satisfied the criteria of the *Sublime* (an eighteenth-century idea of landscape which emphasised the wild untameable strength of nature, as shown in the paintings of Salvator Rosa for example), he now wished for a place which would exemplify the later and rather calmer development of the *Picturesque*. This was the age of the landscape gardener, of Capability Brown and Humphry Repton, and no doubt the Bishop wanted to be in the forefront of the latest movement; after all, he certainly had the means to do so. Repton had written that 'extremes are . . . to be avoided' and nothing could be much more extreme that the situation of Downhill, as anyone can testify who has been there with a wintery northwester blowing. Indeed the Bishop went on in his letter to his daughter to describe the site in appropriate picturesque terms: the distant prospect of Lough Neagh and the Mournes, the

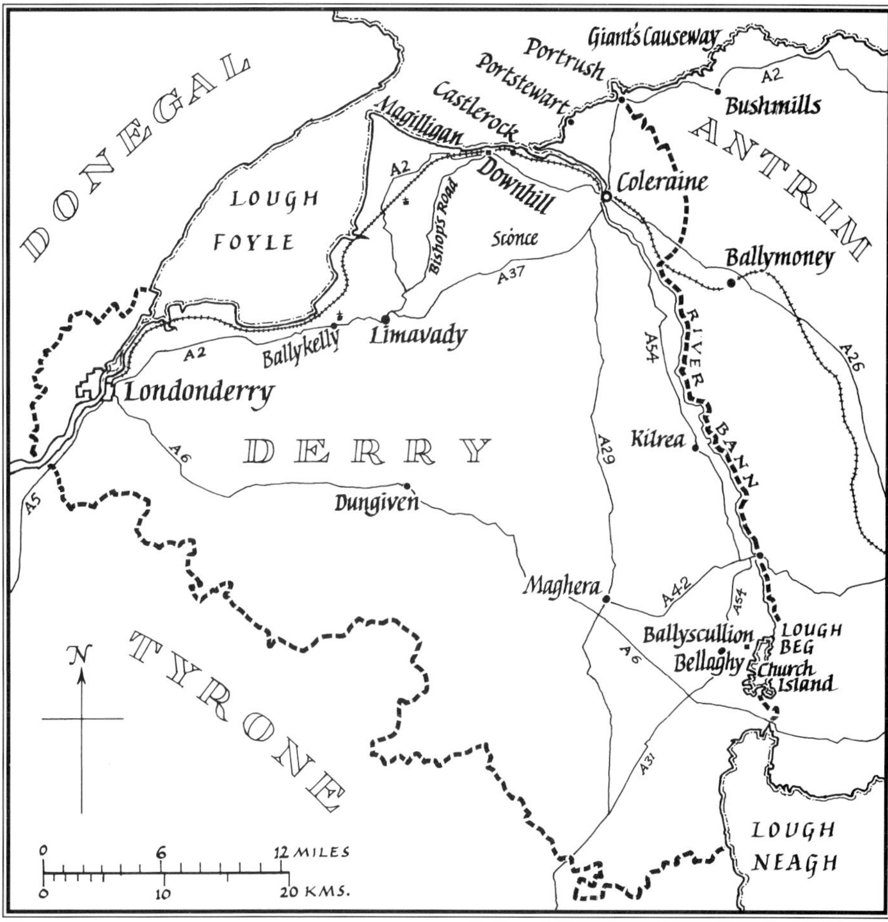

'serpentine River' which will 'decorate the view from my drawing room', Lough Beg itself and then the Bann again to the south 'decorated by Mr O'Neill's new Bridge at Toome', the western view with Derry's woodland Country with an elegant village and the Mansion of Mr Dawson'. As at Downhill, the Bishop conceived of landscapes as framed by the windows of his elegant new rooms. Indeed, the Bishop was quite capable of improving the view himself – though if others could be persuaded to do so, so much the better – and at Ballyscullion he intended to have a bridge built over the Bann at the northern end of the lough (possibly to complement that of Mr O'Neill). In 1792 he was again writing to Mary that 'before the end of the year I hope to have 4 or even 5 spires in the sight of Ballyscullion

VIEW of BALLYSCULLION.

built chiefly at the expence of other people to beautify the prospect.' It is difficult to say whether he had the house in mind as a prospective repository for his rapidly growing art collection, but that is what it surely became as time went by, and the place in which he hoped to put into practice his idea of hanging pictures by schools (see page 79).

Whatever may be said about the Bishop's neglect of his pastoral duties – and he had plenty of critics in that line during his lifetime – this was one of his grand projects which gave a lot of employment and therefore support for the local community. Had he lived in the twentieth century he would have met admirably Hilaire Belloc's requirement that 'It is the duty of the Wealthy Man/ to give employment to the artisan.' When the building work was begun, Shanahan wrote to his employer to say that the neighbourhood would rejoice because they knew 'very well it is the only means to enrich them.'

The faithful Shanahan was once again the main architect -cum-builder-cum-supervisor for the new mansion, though the Bishop had on this occasion an initially clearer idea of what he wanted, having seen a model for it in Belle Isle in Lake Windermere. Belle Isle was a pretty circular building with a domed roof, situated romantically on an island. However it was really only the *idea* of an arcadian temple which was followed, Ballyscullion developing into a larger structure, oval rather than round and with two sweeping wings on either side. The Bishop described it as 'Oval like the Pantheon . . . the Offices joined to the House by a semicircular colonnade like that

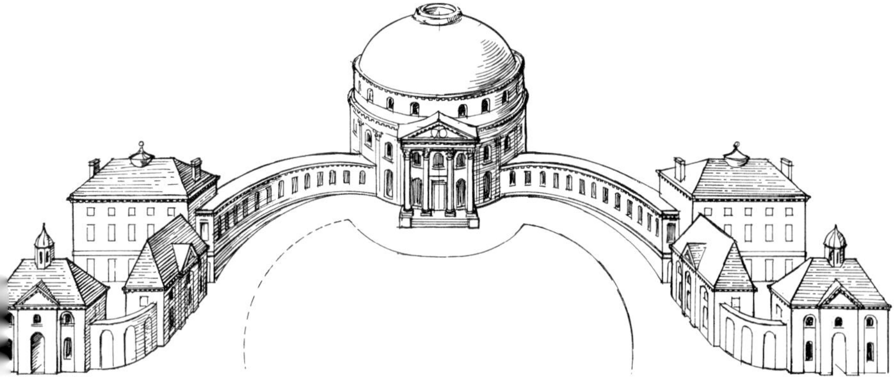

Ballyscullion (left), a rather fanciful engraving from Sampson's Statistical Survey of 1802. (Above) an attempt to make sense of the engraving; the pavilions, whatever their intended form, were never completed and the whole building was dismantled in 1813.

of St Peter's only closed, because of the Climate', displaying both his predilection for curves and the influence of the architecture of Rome, a city which he came to love: 'Tis likewise difficult to say which pleases one most,' he wrote on his third visit, 'the magnificence of ancient or the elegance of modern Rome.' The interior of the house too embodied some new ideas. The hall rose to the full height of the dome, and had bronze-railed galleries connected by a staircase which, according to a *Belfast Newsletter* report of 1787 'is the only thing of its kind in the Kingdom' and 'presents a figure resembling a double corkscrew; a great stair surrounding a lesser one for servants, both so constructed that passengers in one can't perceive those on the other, and forming in their winding ascent communications with every story in the house.' The model for this staircase had come by the Bishop's own admission from Lord Besborough's house at Roehampton (designed by Sir William Chambers) and from the much older example in the great French château of Chambord.

The Bishop had an inscription carved on the cornice around the outside of the house as he had done with the Mussenden Temple (see page 40). This time the text was taken from Virgil, and translates as:

> 'Here is a verdant plain; I will place a temple of marble beside the waters
> Where the vast *Bann* strays in sluggish windings, and clothes his banks with tender reed.'

St George's, Belfast, with the re-erected Ballyscullion portico giving some idea of the scale of the original house.

The river *Bannius* replaced that of *Mincius* in the original Latin. Not everyone felt that the house fitted as well into the landscape as the Bishop had hoped. Sampson, in his 'Statistical Survey' said that Lord Bristol had 'planted a considerable number of trees near Ballyscullion House. They lie too far from the mansion, and are situated too low, to give any additional effect to this princely edifice.' (Sampson does not speculate on how it will all look when the trees are mature.) William Blacker, visiting in 1796 was rather more direct: '. . . at the time I speak of the house appeared as if dropped from the clouds into a large field completely in a state of nature.'

The two 'offices' on either wing were intended for art galleries, with works from the Italian school on one hand, and those of the German on the other, in accordance with the Bishop's new ideas on the educational display of art treasures (see page 79). Samson records seeing some of the Bishop's collection of statuary, including the Apollo Belvedere (see page 86, most likely the cast which the Bishop had been permitted to take by the Pope), the Vatican Mercury and busts of Cicero, Demosthenes, Seneca and Pericles. It may well be that some of these statues are among the fragments which comprise the 'Downhill Marbles', having survived being moved to Downhill and the disastrous fire there in 1851 (see page 147).

Alas, the Bishop was never to fully enjoy Ballyscullion. By the time the building was all but complete he was dead. His successor, the Rev. Henry Hervey Bruce (see page 142), preferred Downhill as a residence and eventually had Ballyscullion 'levelled . . . smack smooth' in the words of Mr Blacker. Bruce apparently moved most of the treasures to Downhill, and what could not be incorporated there was sold. In a fragment of a letter from Lord Londonderry to Bruce in 1805 the former says that some of the Ballyscullion things might suit the house he is building, but the doors would certainly not match. One part of the house which has survived to the present day is the portico from the main entrance; it was purchased by Dr Nathaniel Alexander, the Bishop of Down and Connor, and ended up as the front of St George's Church in Belfast, where it still is. Alexander also bought some columns and mantlepieces for his own houses. Some pink marble columns and some fireplace surrounds went to Port Glenone, Co. Antrim, and some fireplaces also found their way to Bellarena at Magilligan.

It seems sad that this great house built on Irish soil should have vanished so completely. However we can appreciate something of how the house looked by visiting Ickworth in Suffolk; this was the Bishop's last building venture, and can be seen as an expansion and development of the once proud mansion on the shores of Lough Beg. Ickworth, which was only half completed in the Bishop's time, is really Ballyscullion 'writ large'.

Ickworth

THE HISTORY OF ICKWORTH in Suffolk, the Bishop's last and most grandiose building, is every bit as involved and complicated as any of the others. The first moves were made in the summer of 1792 when the Bishop visited the proposed site for this new house in the grounds of his ancestral estates there. He may have considered altering or rebuilding the old family home of Ickworth Lodge at some stage, but changing his mind never seemed to have caused him embarrassment; indeed, his friend Arthur Young said later that the Bishop actually disapproved of the proposed position for the new house; 'he began it while he disliked the spot from the wetness of the soil, and would often tell me that he should never be such a fool as to build in so wet a situation.'

It is not at all clear who was the designer of the great building which emerged, this 'stupendous monument to folly' as his estranged – and perhaps by then embittered – wife was to describe it. The site may have been suggested by Capability Brown who visited the area in 1782; John Soane may have been considered for the work, but having had a brush with the Bishop as a patron once before (see p 28) it is unlikely that he would have accepted even if he had been asked. C. H. Tatham, then a young student in Rome, was apparently given the commission in 1794: 'to my great surprise [the Bishop] consulted me to make him a design for a Villa to be built in Suffolk extending nearly 500 feet, including offices.' Francis Sandys, who had helped out at Ballyscullion, was also present on this occasion, and it was he, together with his brother, who eventually took on the building and oversight of Ickworth; but it was an Italian, one Mario Asprucci the younger, who is credited with the first working designs for Ickworth. These plans show a central rotunda structure with two curved flanking wings terminated with pavilions – a scheme very similar in its essentials to that of Ballyscullion.

Asprucci probably never came to England himself and his design was adopted and modified by the two brothers Sandys, both of whom hailed from the Bishop's see at Derry. Since the Bishop was never present in England at this period, the brothers had to make a papier mâché model of the whole scheme, no doubt intending it to be sent to Italy so that their patron might be kept in touch with developments in Suffolk. Even at that distance the Bishop kept quite a tight rein on the undertaking. He had, for instance, the notion that he felt generally in better form in rooms with very high ceilings; his 'lungs always played more freely . . . spirits spontaneously rose higher in lofty rooms than in low ones, where the atmosphere is too soon tainted with the atmosphere of our own bodies.' The ground floor rooms accordingly reached a height of some 30 feet for the benefit of the Bishop's respiration and also, as he put it, 'of throwing my attick-story (if possible) into St Paul's 3d Heaven.' Perhaps in the Bishop's mind Ickworth was going to rival Wren's St Paul's in London, just as he no doubt felt that the sweeping colonnades would evoke Bernini's piazza at St Peter's in Rome.

His views on the building material were even stronger: writing to his daughter Elizabeth in 1796 on the subject of 'white stone brick' he says,

> 'What! Child, build my house of a brick that looks like a sick, pale *jaundiced* red brick, that would be a red brick if it could, and to which I am certain our posterity will give a little rouge as essential to its health & beauty? White brick always looks as if the bricklayers had not burnt it sufficiently, had been niggardly of the fuel; it looks all dough & no crust.'

As for the 'crust' he commanded stucco facing, according to 'dear impeccable Palladio's rule' – and which has apparently given nothing but trouble ever since. Then there was the matter of the decoration: the original drawings showed a frieze of bas-relief at first floor level of the rotunda, both the sweeping wings, and both the pavilions. These reliefs were to be made by the Italian Carabelli brothers from illustrations from the *Iliad* and *Odyssey* by Flaxman. Flaxman had earlier carried out a sculpture commission for the Bishop (see p 80) not greatly to his own advantage, but it certainly suggests that his patron was very up to date in his taste. To begin with the Bishop had been apprehensive about the cost of having all the subjects carved in relief;

> 'My only difficulty now is how to get the basso-rilievos executed. The upper ones must certainly be painted as Dear Canova sug-

A detail of the Flaxman 'basso-rilievos' at Ickworth.

> gested, being beyond the reach of the eye's accuracy, but the lower ones must be bold and I suppose in gesso . . . As the extent of our basso-rilievos is immense we must blend Oeconomy with our Magnificence or we shall wreck the vessel.'

In the final scheme the reliefs did not feature on either of the wings or flanking pavilions but *did* appear in both the lower and upper bands of frieze round the rotunda. Like the rest of the house, these decorations were not finished until many years after the Bishop's death; the only parts not done by the Carabellis were completed by the Coade Stone works in London, and one design – within the main portico – which may have been designed by Lady Erne's daughter, the Bishop's granddaughter.

As for 'wrecking the vessel' the Bishop, though at some distance from Suffolk, went to some pains to ensure that this should not happen by constantly badgering various of his long-suffering friends to keep an eye on progress. In 1798 he is to be found writing a lengthy letter to an old friend, the Cambridge professor John Symonds, asking him to sort out a disagreement between his 'young hounds' the Sandys brothers on the subject of the relative sizes of the galleries to the domestic offices:

> 'One brother deems that a gallery of 115 feet long will drown my mansion and eclipse its splendour – the other *computes* that less than 115 feet in the length of each gallery will not leave sufficient Room in the square of each office yard for Larders, Laundries,

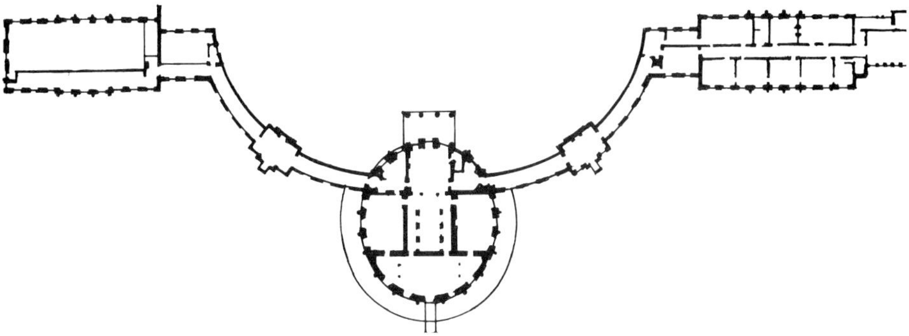

Ground plan of Ickworth

etc., etc., suitable to the Mansion and the family that must inhabit them . . . You on the spot like a true friend examine with your judicious Classical eye the relative proportions of this puzzling animal. Let it be, neither a bustard with wings too small, nor yet a heron with wings too large that drown or eclipse the Body – take if possible Arthur Young with you, that soul of fire, – and be good enough to report to me your deliberate candid advice. . .'

Symonds was also the recipient of the Bishop's ideas on art collection (see the letter quoted on p 79), and it is evident that Ickworth was intended to be a great art gallery as well as a noble mansion; to be 'quite classical – to unite magnificence with convenience & simplicity with Dignity – no redundancy – no superfluity – not one unnecessary Room, but the necessary ones to be noble & convenient; to have few pictures, but choice ones, & my Galleries to exhibit a historical progress of the art of Painting. . .' In other words Ickworth was to have been as Ballyscullion was, only on a grander scale. The grand scale may also have related to the Bishop's grand scheme of the same period of marrying off his youngest son Frederick into the Prussian royal family, and forming thereby a connexion with the Princess of Wales. Had this happened it would have been very useful to be the master of a house sufficiently magnificent for the entertainment of royalty; however Frederick (see p 125) undutifully married a lady of his own choosing.

The Bishop never lived to see this, his greatest project, come to fruition. Most of the art treasure which he had collected for the gal-

The portico at Ickworth, grand enough for even the largest coach to be driven up to the front door.

leries was confiscated during the French occupation of Rome in 1789, and at the time of his death, in 1803, only the central rotunda of the great house was in any way near completion, the flanking wings being merely at the foundation stage. Work on the place then came to a standstill until 1824 when his surviving son, the same undutiful Frederick, began the building again and brought it to a sufficient – though modified – state of completion by 1829 to take up residence there. Ickworth remained in the family until 1956 when it was acquired by the government in lieu of death duties and was subsequently presented to the National Trust.

Today Ickworth is the best place to visit to gain an idea of how high the Bishop's flights of grandeur took him. As well as the great house itself there is as much of the art collection as may be seen in one place. In addition to many of the family portraits, Velasquez, Titian and Poussin are represented and Flaxman's large statue *The Fury of Athamas*, stands in the entrance hall. The portraits (some of which are reproduced in these pages) were painted by many of the most important artists of the eighteenth century: Hogarth, Zoffany, Reynolds, Gainsborough, Vigeé-Lebrun, Batoni, Lawrence and Angelica Kauffmann. The house is furnished and finished in a magnificent manner, and incorporates some of the Bishop's collection of Italian marble chimney pieces – as well as a fine neo-classical one commissioned from Canova. The Bristol family silver ranging in date from the late 1600s to mid-1800s is accounted one of the finest collections in England.

If Ickworth were not the splendid house that it undoubtedly is, it would still be worthy of a visit as in the grounds is the last resting place of the Bishop himself. Some months after his death his remains were interred in the ancestral vault within the family church close to the house. The delay was occasioned by his dying far away in Italy, and one of the more colourful tales about this remarkable man was that, due to the sailor's superstition about the ill-luck of having a corpse on board, the coffin had to be disguised as a packing case and labelled as containing a statue. This in turn led to the legend – not unnaturally – that a statue had been buried in the family vault; the irony of which the man himself would very probably enjoyed. Finally, there is in Ickworth park the memorial obelisk, erected in 1817 by the grateful parishoners of Derry (part of the inscription of which is quoted on p 101), as a remarkable testimony to his abiding popularity there, since he had not set foot in Ireland for at least the last ten years of his life.

The Bishop, painted in Naples by Mme. Vigée-Lebrun in 1790, with Vesuvius smoking in the background.

The Bishop: his personality

IN ANY AGE the Bishop would have been an extraordinary person. In the eighteenth-century there were many larger-than-life personalities competing for places in the first division for the eccentric, but there can be no doubt that Frederick Hervey, fourth Earl of Bristol and Bishop of Derry must have his place there by right; it is also fairly safe to assume that this also was the opinion of his contemporaries. Here are some views of his time:

'This wicked prelate.' – *King George III*

'As brilliant as Lord Chesterfield, but more firmly based.' – *Voltaire*

'Like a shallow stream, rapid, noisy, diverting but useless.' – *Lord Charlemont*

'Entirely easy and unaffeceted in his whole behaviour, exemplary in all parts of worship, plenteous in his good works.' – *John Wesley*

'That mitred Proteus the Count Bishop, who I dare say would be glad of a red hat, and whose crimes you are infinitely too charitable in not seeing in the blackest light, nor can they be palliated but by his profligate folly.' – *Horace Walpole*

'A most excellent companion, pleasant, intelligent, well read, and well bred – liberal minded to the last degree. He has been everywere and knows everything.' – *Jeremy Bentham*

'Lord Bristol is going on like a madman.' – *Lord Hillsborough*

'Though capable of coarseness, had spirit, and was capable, if he wished, to discourse with sensitivity on widely diverse subjects.' – *Wolfgang von Goethe*

'That abominable, wicked old fellow.' – *Lady Holland*

'The idol of his people.' – *William Cole*

> 'An avowed sceptic in religion, the doctrines and institutions of which he would not scruple to ridicule in the company of women . . . 'He is very entertaining and dashes at everything.'
> – *Emma Hamilton*

> 'Most certainly he is a cruel man.' – *Elizabeth Foster* (daughter)

> 'Lord Bristol was one of the most extraordinary men I ever met with.' – *Arthur Young*

Who was right? In a sense all these people were right about him, inasmuch as he was indeed many different things to many different people and truly protean in his ability to change, sometimes quite suddenly. Stories about the Bishop abound, some less creditable than others but all combining to give a picture of a most remarkable man. One of the earliest of these comes from the poet Gray (he of the *Elegy*). Evidently they met when the Bishop had just been appointed to the diocese of Cloyne in 1767: 'I have seen his Lordship of Cloyne often,' he wrote, 'he is very jolly, and we devoured four raspberry puffs together in Cranbourne Alley; but he is gone, and Heaven knows when we shall eat any more.' Evidently he did not stand on his newly acquired dignity too much. Dignity was something he was often able to perceive in others and to deflate if need be. Two often quoted stories concern races which he organised for the benefit of the clergy: having apparently a valuable position to allocate in the Church, he is supposed to have invited the stoutest of his clergy to a large dinner, after which he proposed that they should run a race for the living; the course however took them over some very soft ground where as anticipated they all became stuck, and thus none got the living. On another occasion he arranged an after-dinner horse race between his own clergy and some Presbyterian ministers along Magilligan strand; the Presbyterians won hands down, being by far better horsemen and generally much lighter of build than their portly opposites.

The Bishop was certainly a good horseman himself, favouring this method of travel right up to his 72nd year. His preference for riding rather than the more stately progress of a coach meant that he was able to cover an astonishing amount of ground, and the hundreds of Bristol hotels which are to be seen all over Europe are supposed to derive their names from the idea that the Bishop had

Magilligan strand as it once might have looked; in this old photograph, reproduced from H. J. Bruce's book *Silken Dalliance*, all the post-eighteenth century buildings have been removed – though not the railway.

actually stayed there. (To be fair, it should be said that he did stop at most of the towns and cities where there are such hotels.) His method of travel, *au galop* or 'like a comet' or 'flash of lightening' as it was described, consisted of riding at his own pace while his entourage, 'the clods I bring with me', went on ahead to find accommodation and prepare or command meals; he was used to say 'I arrive provided with the appetite of a curé, but I find the dinner of a bishop.' It was his wont to travel to Italy via the Swiss passes, as his wife (who of course went by carriage) describes in a letter of 1779: '. . . an express arrives from him to let me know he was within a day's journey, very well, very much amus'd, and not the worse from having passed Mt. St. Bernard up to the knees in snow, but that the lame horses retarded him. . .' At this time the Bishop would have been nearly fifty, and it was only later that he would take the coastal route via France as a concession to advancing age. He was a man of whom it could be said that he wished both to travel hopefully *and* to arrive.

Accounts of the Bishop 'at home' give a delightful picture. He was a witty and vivacious character who evidently enjoyed good food, good wine and good company. In 1783 we find him writing to his daughter Mary from Downhill: 'Everything is redolent of Joy and Youth, and we commonly sit down to table from 20 to 25. We have cold Suppers and a bottle of *Champaigne* at each end of the table. The Songsters sing *Ketches*. . .' Proposing and drinking toasts was very much part of the business of dining at Downhill; when many of the Bishop's house guests were poor, but no doubt always hopeful, curates (a long series of rooms in the east wing of the Castle was known as 'the Curates' Corridor') the favourite toast was 'a Rot among the rectors'. This candid wish was apparently coined by a hopeful curate, one Mr Saurin, whose hopes were eventually rewarded when he was made a rector – or so the story goes. When the guests numbered fellow Volunteers the Bishop was inclined to propose 'the Irish Harp restrung'. It would be inaccurate to assume from this that he was a great drinker; in an age when heavy drinking was common among the aristocracy – and had been the downfall of more than one Lord Lieutenant – he was really rather moderate. It had been said of him that 'he would drink a bottle of Madeira like a gentleman' when in company, but it is to be assumed that the bottle was passed around.

That the Bishop enjoyed his wine might be understood from one of his more remarkable and original schemes. Like many gentlemen of the time he bought his claret direct from the grower in Bordeaux, and in 1799 he had the wonderful idea that what he did as an individual, the British government might do on a larger scale; namely to buy up the entire production of Bordeaux at cost price, and then release it in Britain at profit, thus cutting out all the middle men and of course the smugglers. He wrote to his friend Arthur Young:

> 'I imported my Claret at £15 per hogshead [15 gallons], & if you ask Parson Rogers of Sproughton – he can tell you "The Bp. of Derry's wine was a proverb for excellence." Why Government should not export as well as the Bishop of Derry I can not see. And if by a manoeuvre like this they can help you Arthur Young, to drink yr wine at 14d. pr bottle . . . and at the same time put 2 millions clear neat & hard money & ready money into the Exchequer. . .'

The Bishop with his grandchild, Lady Caroline Crichton (Mary's daughter), painted by Hugh Hamilton c.1790. In the background is the English garden of the Villa Borghese which was laid out by the Bishop's protégé Jacob More. The Temple in the distance was designed by Mario Asprucci, the main architect of Ickworth.

The scheme for revenue from wine was but one example of the Bishop's original mind – 'lateral thinking' we might call it today. Another 'Luminous' idea (one of his favourite words) was born in 1782; it was the surprisingly modern notion of raising funds to build a 74-gun battleship by *public subscription*. It got as far as the canvassing of potential sponsors and the drawing up and printing of a subscribers' list, even the servants at Ickworth being solicited ('Lady

Bristol's waiting woman one guinea') for money. In the event a peace treaty was signed between Britain and the United States of America and the immediate need for the ship became less important, and the Bishop's scheme, like so many, was not to be realised.

If making his employees join him in his latest whim represents one side, the autocratic side, of his character, it must be remembered that he could also be disarmingly generous to the people who worked for him. Even towards the end of his life when it seemed that he had become increasingly cranky – in 1801 in Siena he is reported as throwing a tureen of hot pasta out of the window on to a religious procession – he still had the humanity to be kind to old retainers. A year later he was writing home to the diocese which he had not seen for nearly nine years about one 'poor Betty Mcfarland' whose wages he was willing to continue 'while she lives' and about another poor Creature 'who descended to be Kitchen maid – let her in consideration of her zeal remain as such – altho' a more useless domestick in my absence I do not conceive.' There is also a delightful anecdote which probably relates to the building of the back road to Castlerock from Downhill: apparently the wife of one of the servants at the Castle, having given birth to a baby, felt too much in awe of the Bishop's grand establishment to live in with the squalling child lest her husband's employer should be disturbed by it. On learning of the case the Bishop insisted that she would be quite welcome nonetheless; the wife's deference, or timidity, prevailing, the Bishop caused the road to be built in order that she could visit the Castle more easily.

That the Bishop's conversation was as amusing as it was learned we can only know by report. When he met Voltaire on his first trip abroad the old *philosophe* had jestingly pointed out the church and the theatre to the clergyman and asked him in which he thought the greater farce was played; 'that depends on the authors' was the immediate reply. His humour could be wounding as well as unguarded, as his enemies were quick to point out: on one occasion when dining with the King of Prussia, at a time when that country was pursuing a policy of neutrality in Europe, the Bishop refused to have a helping of capon, and on being asked by the King if he disliked it, replied 'Yes, Sir: I have an aversion to all neutral animals.' At other times he was skilled at suiting the action to the word: in 1797 when the Bishop was being heavily criticised at home in Ireland by three Bishops – of probably less wealthy sees – for his lengthy absence from his flock, he sent to the Primate of Armagh three dried peas in an inflated bladder, the traditional attribute of a court jester, with the following tongue twister:

> Three large blue bottles sat upon three blown bladders,
> Blow bottle flies, blow – burst, blown bladders, burst.

The Bishop was also reported as having quite a ribald strain in his talk, though we may guess no more so than was normal among the ruling classes in the century before Victoria came to the throne. In a letter to Emma Hamilton, who perhaps provoked this element in most men whether bishops or not, he wrote thus of the Queen of Naples: 'I verily deem her the very best edition of a woman I ever saw – I mean, of such as are not in *folio* but are to be *had* in *sheets* . . .' Another often repeated story concerns the Bishop leaving Emma's drawing room on the arrival of an acknowledged courtesan, on the grounds that 'it is permitted for a bishop to visit one sinner, but quite unfitting that he should be seen in a brothel.' It is easy to imagine

The fascinating Emma Hamilton, striking a characteristic 'attitude' in Romney's painting.

how people took offence, though the Bishop's manner was surely very light and most of his repartee delivered in a spirit of give and take. Hudson Gurney, an ancestor of the family which became related to the Bishop's successors, the Bruces (see Rosslyn Bruce page 161) gave a good description of the Bishop in Rome and sums up the easiness of his company : 'His table is surrounded by prelates and artists, and his Lordship's wit keeps one in continual laughter the whole time, even in debating serious subjects and saying seriously good things.'

For all his eccentricities, or perhaps because of them, the Bishop had a highly developed sense of humour. The ecclesiastical races on Magilligan have already been mentioned, but his quick wit and oblique sense of the absurd took many other forms. A particularly nice tale concerns his suspicions of certain kinds of extramarital relationships between his staff and his house guests at Downhill. With almost Holmesian ingenuity he is supposed to have sprinkled the corridors with flour last thing at night in order to see where the footsteps led the next morning. We have been left with no evidence as to whether any of the suspected parties came from the Curates' Corridor.

Much has been written about the Bishop's mode of dress. He caused something of a stir in Rome in 1779 by wearing the full canonicals of an English Bishop to attend a religious ceremony in the Sistine Chapel. Often he was described as wearing purple as though such a colour were extraordinary in itself; when he ordered material for clothing he usually described it as 'puce' which sounds much less garish. Truly spectacular, and intended to be so, was the costume he adopted to attend the Dublin Volunteer Convention in 1783 (see page 98) – episcopal purple with gold-laced white gloves and the military hat of a colonel of the Volunteers. The mixture of clerical and soldierly garb was also noticed when he passed through Oxford in 1785; 'a light lilac coat and his Volunteer hat fiercly cocked, laced, and with a cockade' brought forth the exclamation from an onlooker, 'why sure, Thomas, that there man cannot be a parson in them there clothes'. It must be added that in all his surviving portraits the Bishop appears to be very soberly and decently dressed, most usually in the conventional black of a minister of the established Church. He often gave fine material for clothing as presents, an unusual but very practical way of showing favour.

The Bishop's art collection

MORE OR LESS as soon as he had the means to do so, the Bishop began to collect art objects, and for a man whose detractors claimed could not stick at any one thing for any length of time it became a passion which lasted him for the rest of his life. By 1780 the Downhill Castle was being extended northwards from its original trim design and one of the wings thus formed was required to house the growing collection of paintings and statuary. By 1783 it had to be extended by another 'New' gallery which suggests something of the speed at which the Bishop was amassing his treasures.

As the collection grew, so did the Bishop's rather advanced ideas of housing it which he developed at Downhill, through Ballyscullion to Ickworth. Here, in a letter to his friend John Symonds, he sets out the idea:

> The idea I have struck out of showing the historical progress of the art of Painting in all the *five* different schools of Germany & Italy I deem both happy & instructive. Galleries in general are both confused & uninstructive. Mine, by classing the authors under the different schools, will show the characteristick Excellence of each, instruct the young mind & edify the old.

Venice	*Bologna*	*Roman*	*Florence*	*Naples*
Coloring	*Composition*	*Sentiment*	*Drawing*	*Extravagance*
Titian	*Guido*	*Rafael*	*M. Angelo*	*Salvator Rosa*

If the Bishop's idea of an art gallery being a means of education (rather then the old treasure-room, *kunstkammer* idea) seems surprisingly modern, his choice of collected work is also remarkable in its breadth and catholic (with a small 'c') taste. He was interested, on the one hand, in the pre-Renaissance period which he referred to as the 'Fine old pedantry of painting', and is recorded as having acquired a Cimabue, a thirteenth century artist not greatly valued at that time but greatly considered now. He was also a champion of Albrecht Dürer, 'Divine Homerican Albert Dürer', again a taste which might have been thought 'barbaric' by some in the eighteenth century. Then, on the other hand, he was fully abreast of contemporary leanings in the world of art, taking up and commissioning young artists, often at the beginning of their careers. The young sculptor Flaxman was a case in point: he met the Bishop in Rome in about 1790 and immediately made a strong impression: 'Who will probably rise to be the first Sculptor in Europe – exquisite *Canova* not excepted,' was the Bishop's verdict on the young man who, though at that time not yet fully recognised, was soon to become one of the movers of Neo-Classicism in Europe. The Bishop commissioned a hugely ambitious sculpture from him, a work which he welcomed initially with great enthusiasm; 'I cannot conclude my letter without telling you the liberality of Lord Bristol has reanimated the fainting body of Art in Rome.' But before he had completed the sculpture he came to realise that the sum he had asked for (£600) was much too little. However the piece, *The Fury of Athamas*, was a success and was one of the few of Flaxman's full-scale sculptures to survive; today it can be seen at Ickworth. Ickworth is also decorated on the outside with two friezes of bas-relief from Flaxman's designs.

The Fury of Athamas, by Flaxman.

For the most part, the contemporary artists who benefited most from the Bishop's patronage were portraitists. The Bishop sat for his own portrait several times to the first artists of the day: the fashionable Italian artist Batoni painted him in his clerical robes and with a view of Derry Cathedral in the background in 1777/8. Then a charming portrait was made in 1790 by Vigée-Lebrun while at Naples, and this time the background is supplied by a smoking Mount Vesuvius. In the same year he was also painted by Angelica Kauffmann (who was the first woman member of the Royal Academy in Rome), a slightly less animated likeness, with the Bishop looking rather weary beneath a classical bust of Maecenas, the allusion being to the concept of artistic patronage. It has been suggested that the vivacity of the first picture by comparison with the second was in part due to the fact that the first artist was young, French and pretty, but that the other was Swiss and of maturer years. Angelica Kauffmann also painted a fine portrait (now at Ickworth) of the Bishop's daughter Elizabeth.

Commissions were also granted to less famous names. The landscape painter Thomas Jones was taken up by the Bishop while in Naples with the Hamiltons, and he not only sold his pictures to the Bishop but also painted them to order. Another such was Jacob More, who met the Bishop in Italy in 1778. More carried out many commissions, most of which found their way to Downhill in due course. (In 1786 there arrived at Downhill '6 Landscapes by More on large paper in Watercolours very beautiful.') More came to work for the Bishop in another capacity, that of artistic agent, and this involved the buying and shipping of pictures, prints, drawings, statues, casts and even mosaic pavement. Before the French wars the amount of treasure which was exported was colossal, and a large part of it went directly by sea from Italy to Derry to be installed in the Castle. More was not the only one empowered to purchase *objets d'art* for the Bishop; there was also a Mr Hope, working for him in Amsterdam, and he was not above persuading members of his family to search out specific items for him, especially his daughter Mary. Here he is in 1792 writing from Plymouth concerning some pictures which he narrowly missed collecting in Rome:

'Commission on Commission, my dearest Mary . . . I have set my heart upon 2 pictures to be sold at Christie's in Pall Mall on Satur-

Moon Light, Diana bathing, with Nymphs by Jacob More, 1786. Despite featuring a clifftop temple and a dedication to the Bishop, More's engraved work did not apparently appeal to his patron.

> day the 24th which I actually did buy in my last séjour at Rome, & was jockey'd from by the Vendor pretending after 3 days receipt of my money that he meant Pounds sterling and not zecchins – eh che differenza, Mia Cara!

In fact the Bishop did not manage to acquire these pictures even on the second attempt, despite Mary's efforts. Mary also gained permissions to excavate antique pieces from the Forum in Rome, in which activity a mutual interest would most certainly have been held by the Bishop's old friend Sir William Hamilton. Hamilton, who had known the Bishop since his schooldays, was the English Envoy to the Court of Naples and shared with the Bishop a lifelong interest in collecting art objects and specifically ancient Greek and Roman fragments.

So it was that from all these sources works of art flowed into Ireland, destined initially for 'the Downhill which I flatter myself will be a Tusculanium' as the Bishop put it, and then, when that house was no longer large enough to accommodate them, for the next of his 'Galleries', Ballyscullion. The flow continued fairly steadily until it was abruptly checked in 1798 when the French invaded Rome and seized the mass of the Bishop's collection there, a collection which he claimed was worth between 18 and £20,000, and which he spent much of the remainder of his life attempting to reclaim ('. . . all that immense & valuable & beautiful property of large mosaick pavement, sumptuous chimney pieces for my new house, & pictures, statues, busts & marbles without end, first rate Titians & Raphaels, dear Guidos, and three old Caraccis – gran Dio che tesoro – ') Some of his treasures had been got away by his bankers in Leghorn (Livorno) before the French advance and had gone by sea to Naples. However, the pieces rescued were apparently not the most valuable, and the Bishop was greatly vexed with his lawyers for being panicked into paying £1,800 for the transport of goods which he only valued at £670!

The loss of such a large part of his collection did not restrain him at all in his urge for new acquisitions after the defeat of the French; if anything it appears to have stimulated it further, for in 1803, the year of the Bishop's death, he was reported as spending about £5,000 a quarter on works of art. On his death, a friend in Rome intervened to prevent his property there from disappearing an second time, and the effects which remained were valued at £14,000. Even though the Bishop was devoting these colossal sums to the collection of art, he was ever anxious to make a saving where he could, to the extent of evading a little import duty; to the Rev. Henry Hervey Bruce, his factotum at Downhill, he wrote in 1801, '*Pictures & Statue.* Ask the Collector of Derry, & Him of Coleraine whether he will allow me, as Sr. Hugh Hill did, to import my Pictures as Canvass & my Statue as Marble.'

Such then was the background of all the treasures which came to Ireland for the great houses at Downhill and Ballyscullion, and then latterly to Ickworth in Suffolk. Since there has not survived any kind of definitive inventory, we can not be sure of exactly what the collection may have comprised in its heyday. Some items have survived and some have been documented, and by listing some of these few an idea can be obtained of the size and quality of the original assembly.

Many of the portraits and other pictures commissioned by the

A marble bust of the Bishop, by Hewetson, c.1778.

Bishop may be seen today at Ickworth. His own picture, by Vigée-Lebrun hangs there in the drawing room, between two famous Gainsborough portraits, one of his brother Augustus John Hervey, and the other of his eldest son, Lord Hervey. Angelica Kauffmann's portrait of the Bishop is also there, as is a small bust of him by the Irish sculptor Christopher Hewetson, and he appears in a curious picture he commissioned from William Hoare of Bath, where he is shown presenting his eldest son to the Earl of Chatham – an event which almost certainly could not have happened. Finally, he is portrayed by Hugh Douglas Hamilton in a pretty pastel, with a panorama of Rome in the background.

We know that some of the pictures now at Ickworth were formerly at Downhill, the Kauffmann portrait of the Bishop and the William Hoare group, for example. Other works, such as a fine Titian and a landscape by Poussin may also have originally hung at Downhill. Some of the works at Downhill are known only because of short lists compiled by Neale, and by Sampson in 1802; about 50 pictures are mentioned, including Raphael, Rembrandt and Titian.

The largest of these would certainly have been Guido Reni's *Aurora*, sometimes called 'The Division of Light from Darkness', which was placed in the ceiling of the main gallery at Downhill in 1783 (see page 14). This picture was a copy, the original being in Rome, and it was destroyed in the disastrous fire the house suffered in 1851. A contemporary account noted the loss of some of the other pictures, including a 'Boar Hunt' by Raphael, but many were apparently carried to safety.

The statuary was not so lucky, being less transportable, and much of it was very badly damaged or destroyed. A survivor of the statue collection was the 'Child and Dolphin' which the Bishop valued greatly and believed to be by Raphael (it is now thought to be the work of Nollekens) and which can be still seen at Ickworth. It would seem that, after the 1851 fire, many of the damaged pieces and fragments were deposited – 'dumped' might be a more appropriate word – in the area immediately outside the south wall of the rose garden, close beside where the car park is today. Such pieces that survive were collected by the warden in the 1960s and were then arranged in the crypt of the Temple. Subsequently this collection has been partially dispersed, some of it being stored in Hezlett House (see page 184) until a permanent display can be arranged. Of these pieces, some nine have been identified positively as being ancient Roman, dating from the first and second centuries AD and it is very likely that they would have been excavated from Rome. These 'Downhill Marbles' were identified by Professor Jocelyn Toynbee in 1965 and are remarkable survivals. Many of the Bishop's ancient treasures probably came from Rome where a good deal of excavation was taking place in the latter part of the eighteenth century. During one visit he wrote home:

> 'for my own part I have been singularly fortunate – several ancient rooms have been unearth'd since my arrival – the paintings were in fresco & almost as perfect as at first – the secret was soon found of detaching the painted stucco from the walls, & I have bought three complete rooms, with wch I purpose to adorne the Downhill & le rendre un morceau unique ...'

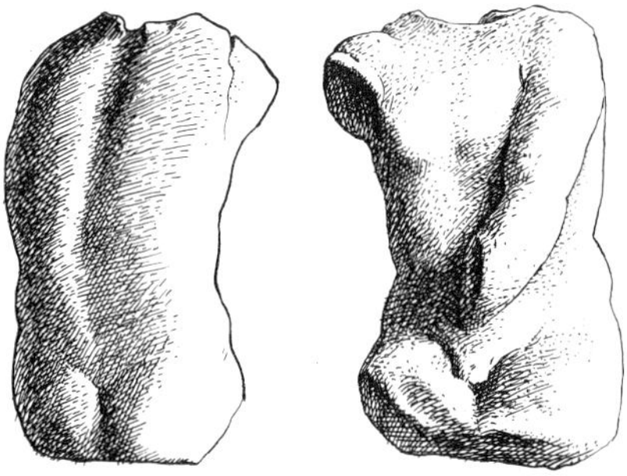

A Roman Torso

A sculpted fragment, possibly of one of the 'Consuls'.

Quite how classical Roman wall paintings might have been used to 'adorne' the Castle is a matter for conjecture. Statuary removed from the Forum and other sites was more easy to accommodate.

There were also many fragments of eighteenth-century statues, among which are the remaining 'ounce' from the Lion Gate, and a strong contender for the head of the van Nost statue of the Bishop's brother George. Other pieces include fragments of casts of classical and neo-classical works, which the Bishop would have probably referred to as 'gesses' (i.e. made with gesso). Through Shanahan's letters we know that there was a statue of Apollo in the 'New Gallery', and this was probably a copy of the Apollo Belvedere, which the Bishop had obtained permission to take a cast from in 1777. Evidently it had suffered in transit: 'On examining the statues in the gallery, I find that of Apollo wanting the nudities and three fingers, and that of one of the consuls three fingers and a thumb'. Sampson's survey reported a statue both of the Apollo Belvedere and the Vatican Mercury in Ballyscullion at a later date and it is known that the Bishop also had a copy of the Laocöon group there as well. Shanahan's reference to 'consuls' may correspond with Sampson's later description of Cicero, Demosthenes, Seneca and Pericles. It is worth remembering that when the Rev. Henry Hervey Bruce inherited the Bishop's possessions he closed Ballyscullion (not wishing to pay window tax on a house in which he had no intention

Cavaceppi's centaur, sculpted in *c.*1768, transported to Downhill in 1791 and sited in front of the Castle until the 1940s.

of living) and many of the treasures there would have been removed to Downhill, after the sale of 1813.

One of the most impressive pieces of sculpture was the famous centaur which stood against the double flight of steps to the main south entrance to the Castle. This very fine work was by the sculptor and 'antique restorer' Bartolomeo Cavaceppi and was modelled on one of a pair of centaurs which had been found in Hadrian's Villa in the 1730s. The Bishop intended the centaur for Ballyscullion, and it is known that it took the combined efforts of ten men to move the piece there from Belfast in 1791. Evidently Bruce had the centaur brought back to Downhill in the early nineteeth century, where it survived the fire of 1851 – being described in a contemporary account as 'grinning with delight at the ruin and devastation by which it was surrounded' – and where it remained until the 1940s. There was an auction at the Castle when the Bruce family finally left in 1921 but the centaur stayed, partly because of a valuation at the time of £5,000, until bought by Sir Basil Macfarlane in 1940 and taken to a new home in Aberfoyle House, Derry. Finally this remarkable sculpture came to be auctioned at Sotheby's in April of 1988 where it went in a blaze of glory for £55,000 to an unidentified buyer, and despite enquiries its whereabouts are now a secret.

Besides the classical remains and eighteenth century pieces at Downhill there are also many fragments of the interior decoration of the house which give a good idea of the very high standard of the general workmanship. These include some of the little plaster rosettes which formed the decoration of the inside of the dome of the Temple. Many pieces are difficult to identify, and it may even be that some are from either of two copies of the Warwick Vase known to have been in the Castle at the time of Sampson's survey. The orig-

The Warwick vase; the Castle contained two copies

Marble bust by Massei, thought to be of Sir Robertson Bruce.

inal vase, which is now in the Burrell Collection in Glasgow, was excavated from a lake near to Hadrian's Villa by Gavin Hamilton, a dealer and artist but no relation of the Bishop's lifelong friend Sir William Hamilton, who bought the pieces and had them reconstituted. The vase then became the most important piece in his own collection and it is almost certain that the Bishop would have seen it during one of his frequent visits to Naples, and was then no doubt fired with the idea of having a replica of his own for Downhill.

Other sculptures associated with Downhill include a portrait bust, thought to be of Sir Robertson Bruce, the second baronet and the only one of the family to bear the title without the Christian name Hervey, and a fine marble portrait bust by Turnerelli of Lord Liverpool, husband of the Bishop's third daughter, Louisa.

The Bishop as an amateur scientist

THE EIGHTEENTH CENTURY has been dubbed the 'Age of Enlightenment' as a product of the burgeoning of scientific discovery at that period. The Bishop saw himself very much as part of the movement of the time, and both his first and last expeditions to the Continent took in a certain amount of this interest.

In 1765 the Bishop set off with his family on the *Grand Tour* of Europe, a trip which in the following year brought him to Naples (where his old schoolfriend William Hamilton was the British Envoy) to see a promised eruption of the volcano Vesuvius. Hamilton himself was deeply interested in the phenomenon and his enthusiasm must have rubbed off on his guest. In March the mountain duly obliged and the Bishop was one of a party which ascended the side to observe more closely the flow of lava. Whether the Bishop got too close or was merely unlucky, he was hit on the arm by a red hot stone thrown up by the eruption. Afterwards he wrote of his experience to his daughter Mary:

> '. . . we found a great hollow of about forty feet & half a mile round: at the bottom of this were two large mouths from whence the mountain frequently threw up two or three hundred red hot stones some as big as your head, and some considerably larger; one of these struck me on the right arm, and without giving me much pain at the time made a wound about two inches deep, tore my coat all to shreads, & by a great effusion of blood alarm'd my companions more than myself.'

The wound did not mend very quickly and kept him in bed for over a month, but it did nothing to deter his interest in all things to do with volcanoes, an interest which lasted all his life.

Four years after this episode he is writing to his nephew Phipps about his geological discoveries, 'You have doubtless heard much of our Giant's Causeway: till lately it had been reckoned single of its kind, but I have lately discover'd such varieties of the same sort both in France and Italy.' He was particularly fascinated by the Giant's

A miniature of the Bishop, painted by an unknown Italian artist, *c.*1792. Vesuvius features in the background, and the Bishop appears to be holding an elevation of Ballyscullion or Ickworth.

Causeway (it has been said that he chose Downhill as the site for his house having seen it when riding from Derry to inspect the Causeway) and was passionate about any area where such 'polygonal Basaltes' were to be found. At the start of his interest Shanahan was detailed to make drawings of things which bore on the subject; '*Sugar-loaf* or Conical Mountains . . . Granite, Chrystal, or Petrified Shells, or Pumice Stone.' Later he enlisted the help of an Italian, Bitio, to do this work, often sending him off on his own to make drawings in volcanic areas such as the Auvergne in France. It was not really Shanahan's forte, but he did it 'to please his Lordship' (see page 23).

A fireplace mantle from Downhill Castle constructed from a mosaic of different stones of geological interest.

Bitio, who was primarily an artist rather than an architect, was much more the man for the job, although the Bishop reckoned that he was not at his best when he put people in his work: 'his men are beasts and his beasts brutes'. However his draughtsmanship was good enough otherwise to satisfy his critical patron and he was even sent to Ireland to make scientific drawings there – a far cry from his native Belluno in the Veneto, exchanging, as Mrs Hervey put it, rice and *uccelli* for beef and claret. Writing to John Strange at this time he reports that Bitio had drawn 'a very accurate view of the Mountains of Mourne, which greatly resemble our Paduan hills'. Strange, who was both a diplomat (British Envoy to Venice) and a qualified scientist, was a frequent correspondent, and remained one of the Bishop's friends for many years.

The Bishop's concern with 'Volcanick matters' in the early and middle parts of his life helped to establish the relationship of geological features such as the Giant's Causeway and the caves of Staffa and indeed many similar sites in Europe and the Mediterranean; his travels did not take him to visit Santorini and other Greek islands but his protean way of thinking led him easily to suppose that the volcanic common denominator would relate them to Derry and Antrim. When he built Downhill he filled it with fine fireplaces of different kinds of marble, partly chosen for their aesthetic qualities but partly, we may be sure, for their scientific associations; as he put it 'any specimens of Volcanic matter, among which I reckon all sorts of Chrystallizations and Vitrifications, all Granites and Porphyries'. Even towards the end of his life in the 1790s this hobby was very much alive with him. Writing to Sir William Hamilton from Siena in July of 1794, he is in a high state of excitement about an extraordinary 'rain' of volcanic stone during a violent thunderstorm:

> The stones are of a quality not found in any other part of the Sienese territory; they fell about 18 hours after the enormous eruption of Vesuvius, which circumstance leaves choice of difficulties in the solution of this extraordinary phenomenon. – either these stones have been generated in the igneous mass of clouds which produced such unusual thunder, or, which is equally incredible, they were thrown from Vesuvius at a distance of at least 250 miles – judge then of its parabola.'

For a man whom contemporaries reckon was not a 'stayer', his enthusiasms for these matters seem to have been rather well maintained.

The Bishop had other, and some might say more practical, scientific leanings as well. He advocated the use of lime on the land in his diocese; it is possible that the inspiration for this came from his friend and correspondent the economist Arthur Young who, writing of the Bishop's lands, said that 'he did all he could to improve it for his tenants. With an interest in chemistry he started burning lime to put on the land'. The Bishop himself described the purpose in a slightly more poetic terms: 'Lime stone at the bottom & turf at the top what gold may not be in this chemistry produce' – the 'gold' of this agricultural alchemy being grain crops, a relative newcomer in a country whose staple was traditionally the potato.

Projects for the improvement of farming methods were always close to the Bishop's heart; he felt that Science should be the servant of the farmer, thus in 1774 we find him writing 'Tis a pity likewise that mechanical powers are not more extensively studied that our country squires and country clergy might be the better able to remove the gross ignorance of our country farmers.' He thought that 'all the implements of husbandry are so ignorantly constructed that the works of husbandry are made doubly expensive.' Accordingly we find him writing to Arthur Young some years later to say that he had 'sent 20 of yr swingling ploughs over to my Tenant at the Downhill', adding pessimistically 'but I fear they will draw them by the Horses tails.' For his own lands he also designed neat oaken gates. In Derry he promoted and encouraged coal-mining. In 1768, when he was given the freedom of the City of Londonderry, it was reported that among other achievements he had caused the establishment of a colliery.

The Bishop was similarly interested in underground rivers and did much investigation of them while in Italy, writing to his friend Strange in 1771 that he had 'visited almost every subterraneous river in Istria' and advancing some rather extreme suggestions that rivers which go underground in Greece might rise in Sicily! At Downhill he contented himself with the creation of fishponds (see page 56) and a cascade, but towards the end of his life he devoted much energy to a very grand scheme for draining the Pontine Marshes, a scheme which he hoped would be adopted by the Queen of Naples and bring to the kingdom a great deal of much needed revenue. The plan came to nothing.

Astronomy was yet another preoccupation, though it is to be inferred, not a long lasting one. A large telescope was ordered for Downhill from the celebrated astronomer William Herschel. At the end of 1790 Herschel wrote to the Bishop to inform him that the 20 foot reflector was well under construction at Slough in England and that it would be set up for testing in the spring prior to delivery, should he wish to see it in action. The letter asked for details of the kind of clock the Bishop was going to use in conjunction with the instrument, and gives instructions for the sort of plinth which would be required for mounting it in Ireland. Whether the project was beginning to look rather expensive (Herschel also mentions an advance of two or three hundred pounds) or that the astronomical fit was passing, it seems unlikely that the telescope was ever delivered; the letter is endorsed by the Bishop, 'Begged to postpone.'

Science in the eighteenth century was perhaps more of a liberal art and less narrowly specialised that it is today, so there is nothing very surprising in finding him meeting on equal terms with 'real' or experimental scientists of his epoch, such as D'Anville or Benjamin Franklin. If not a great practitioner of the sciences he was certainly a great *amateur*, and as such was accorded the honour of being elected as a fellow of the Royal Society in 1782.

The Bishop as a politician

IN THE BISHOP'S TIME matters of state and faith were as inextricably bound up together as they have been ever since in Ireland. At the start of his episcopal career he threw himself into the affairs of Anglo-Irish politics with a great deal of energy, which, like so many of his cherished projects, only began to wane when he found that he was unable to change the *status quo* singlehanded or overnight. His interest may have waned from time to time but, just as with his interest in more general and European politics, it never left him entirely.

The Bishop's family had traditionally supported the Whigs and though, like so many others before and since, he became more right wing in his views in old age, this also was his view in the first half of his life. Initially the ability to walk with kings yet have the common touch was quite naturally part of his character; on being appointed to the see of Derry, one of the richest in Ireland, at the age of only thirty-seven, one of his first public acts was to ride around every parish within his jurisdiction to make sure that all his clergy were appropriately housed. At the same time he set up a fund for the support of 'retired' curates. It was a good start, especially in the eyes of the ordinary people who were more used to having bishops who behaved like absentee landlords. Dean Swift, who understood Ireland better than many, produced the most telling, albeit facetious explanation for the general quality of bishop the country was normally destined to receive: his theory was that the newly London-appointed clerics were invariably ambushed by highwaymen on Hounslow Heath as they made their way westwards to take up their new posts. The rogues and cut-throats, having relieved the new bishops of both their purses and their letters-patent would then proceed to Ireland in their stead. Bishop Frederick Hervey did not fall into this category however, and he quickly became a popular figure in his diocese not only for the liberality of his purse but also for the liberality of his ideas.

That the Bishop could be all things to all men may be neatly illustrated through the remarks of Horace Walpole, who was bitterly opposed to the Bishop's 'preposterous idea' of widening the franchise, when he maintained that had there been any Mohammedans in the diocese they too would have been given the vote! With hindsight we might reasonably suppose that the Bishop would have at least donated money for the building of a mosque, in the same way that he dispensed sums for building to both Presbyterian and Catholic alike, as can be judged from contemporary accounts and receipts. In 1784 he donated £210 (200 guineas) to the building of the Roman Catholic chapel in Derry, in 1785 £50 went to Mr Knox for his Presbyterian Meeting House in Articlave (the Bishop also assisting in laying the foundation stone), in 1787 £22 15s. went towards the Roman Catholic chapel in Desertmartin, and £11 7s. 6d. for the Macosquin Meeting House near Coleraine. Nor was charity reserved for home: in 1781 he presented 50 guineas to the building of the first Presbyterian church in Belfast and on another occasion, while riding through the parish of Saul in Down, he noticed a chapel lacking a roof and immediately sought out the priest to present him with £10 to help finish the work. In addition, when the new parish church at Tamlaghtard was built, probably about 1874, the Bishop offered the old building to the Roman Catholics. (A tomb said to be that of St Aidan can be seen today by the ruins of this old church; nearby is a holy well, and the R. C. church of St Aidan of 1826.)

Money flowed fairly readily when the results could be seen in bricks and mortar, but it was also forthcoming for less tangible matters. When the Bishop first came to Derry he donated £1,000 to a fund for the widows of the clergy and an annual sum of £16 to the poor of that city, besides benefiting many individuals who petitioned him personally. It can be argued that the Bishop could well afford to be bountiful but no one could deny that he took a very lively interest in the use to which wealth was put as well as the power and influence it gave him.

One of the most truly ecumenical uses of his influence was in that of trying to procure a fairer deal for the Catholics, not only within his own see but in Ireland as a whole. One basic iniquity in the Bishop's eyes was embodied in the Oath of Allegiance to George III which Catholic clergy could not take because its form denied the authority of the Pope, and thus Catholics could not occupy any decision-making positions in the legislature. When a new act, the 'Test Act', was made law in 1774 it was viewed largely as an early if tentative step in favour of Catholics because, theoretically, it enabled them to take the oath without compromising their consciences. The Bishop had worked very hard towards this legislation, even so far as conferring with the Pope in 1771 on the subject. However, the result was disappointing as few in Ireland availed themselves of it and finally Rome did not sanction it.

Another area in which the Bishop busied himself was one which affected Presbyterians as well as Catholics. He regarded as an 'injustice' and a 'horrid local grievance' the fact that these two groups had to pay tithes to the minister of the established Church, 'paying a teacher he does not hear'. The Bishop's reforming scheme was based on the exchange of the tithe for land of the same value, that value to be arbitrated by a committee assembled by the local sheriff. It was agreed by the Church authorities that the idea could be tried experimentally in Derry, but somehow nothing ever came of it.

It was in the matter of the Volunteer Movement that the Bishop devoted the most continuous of his efforts. The Volunteers had been started in 1778 in response to fears about Britain's ability to protect Ireland from the threat of a foreign invasion; America and France being the countries most to be feared at the time. (In course of time France became the real worry, and it is a matter of speculation whether the formidable looking castellated walls which were added to Downhill about 1875 were merely intended as a 'picturesque' addition or were meant to present the appearance of a clifftop fortress from the sea.) The Bishop threw himself wholeheartedly into Volunteer affairs; in about 1783 he was made a colonel of the Londonderry Corps and it has been said that he presented it with some artillery with 'O Lord open thou our lips and our mouths shall shew forth thy praise' engraved on the barrels. Whereas the Bishop saw the Volunteers and his position within the movement as a means to forward much needed reforms, the British government saw it as a dangerous and possibly subversive organisation and for some time had the Bishop shadowed by spies. The Bishop thought that if he could only win the overall leadership of the Volunteers he might be able to push through various pieces of legislation including that of extending the vote to the Catholics. In this as in other things he came into conflict with the commander-in-chief, the plodding and cautious Lord Charlemont. To begin with the Bishop seemed to carry all before him and at the second Dungannon Convention of the Volunteers in 1783 his ideas received a full vote of thanks.

However at the main Convention in Dublin later in the same year, he was to be outmanoeuvred by Charlemont's more moderate element. The Bishop understood well the importance of public appearances and his entry into Dublin for the Convention was stage-managed with great panache: dressed in purple and white with diamond shoe and knee buckles he progressed through the city in an open landau in truly regal fashion, preceded by his notorious nephew George 'Fighting' Fitzgerald (see page 138) at the head of a squadron of Dragoons in scarlet and gold uniforms, surrounded by liveried postillions and followed by further squadrons of military horsemen. Fanfares of trumpets and the presentation of arms by the guard of honour marked his arrival at the Parliament buildings. This ostentatious display was rapturously received by the populace but it did not greatly impress the delegates and when, following much oratory and scheming, the Convention was finally wound up after 20 days virtually nothing that the Bishop had hoped for had been achieved. The last hope of any kind at all for Parliamentary reform had been formulated by Henry Flood, whom the Bishop had supported, but was heavily defeated when presented to the Irish Commons. Even had this bill been adopted, it contained no relief for the Catholic community. The Bishop returned to Derry somewhat embittered by the whole procedure and consoled himself with delivering strongly worded addresses to various post-convention assemblies: 'The representatives of mean, corrupt, decayed and depopulated boroughs, to a man almost, were against us' he wrote to the Drogheda Association; 'The present House of Commons, even if they were a legitimate body, are certainly the servants & not the masters of the People' to the Londonderry Volunteers; 'May the armed citizens of Ireland therefore imitate their prototypes the armed citizens of Rome' to the Strabane Battalion; and to that of Coleraine, 'But as our ancestors, gentlemen, wrenched the Constitution from the tyrannical grip of one part of the legislature, 'tis now become the duty of their Posterity to rescue it from the corrupt hands of the other.' It was all very much fighting, if not to say revolutionary talk, and it is hardly surprising that the powers in Westminster and Dublin felt threatened by such sentiments, especially as they were coming from a man who was both a bishop and an English nobleman. The Bishop was never again to be so deeply and personally involved in the politics of his adopted country; perhaps the fail-

The 'Episcopal Volunteer', a caricature of the Bishop in haranguing mode.

ure of this essay discouraged him from being quite so active again with the Volunteers; perhaps he realised, as he might have done at the outset, that success for his particular reforms was unlikely insofar as the Volunteers had quickly become, from its foundation, an exclusively Protestant body. On the other hand optimism always seems to have marked his attitude, especially when in the full flight of a fresh enthusiasm.

The Bishop was also greatly absorbed by events on the continent of Europe. Even with the Napoleonic Wars raging and the final outcome in no way settled, he was busy with schemes to divide up the world anew. One such was to divide France in half, the northern bit to go to the Republicans, the southern to the Monarchists, thus neatly emasculating the one nation which was the greatest military threat to Britain. At the same time Holland, 'a blackguard, mean, low, shabby, rival power', was to be broken up into small provinces and given to various parts of the yet to be united Germany, thus removing Britain's main commercial rival. In all his latter travels the Bishop quite unashamedly acted in the rôle of an amateur spy, constantly writing to his old friend Sir William Hamilton, the British Envoy to Naples, with political and military intelligence from wherever he happened to be. Thus in 1794 he writes from Trieste that the French have a 'whole fleet of transports, gun-boats, and all, are under weigh for Venice; the wind is neither favourable or strong, But in two days they hope to reach it. . .' In 1799, writing to Lord Liverpool from Ratisbon, he is full of the possibilities of mounting an invasion of Brittany with the help of the loyalist natives, 'That the Chouans are still superior to the Republican troops & that upon the appearance of an English army & especially as large an one as 30 or 40,000 men, that province and Normandy & the famous Vendée cd easily be raised many more'. (The *Chouans*, or Breton monarchists, still exist; these days they tend to be tattooed and leather-jacketed young men.) It is more than likely that it was this kind of correspondence which led to the Bishop's arrest and imprisonment in the fortress at Milan for about nine months between 1798 and 1799. Far from deterring him from his information gathering activities, he actually managed to carry on with them while still in detention, quizzing and soliciting military intelligence from the French officers who visited, and those who were charged with guarding him – though it must be added that he was still able to live in quite a grand style during this spell. Almost immediately after his release he is to be found writing both to Hamilton and to Lord Nelson, imparting all his gleanings from Milan, and especially recommending that a naval attack on Toulon might be carried out successfully due to the poor condition of the port's defences: 'The *Garrison* was composed of a few hundred Invalids – the guns of old bad Iron, on rotten carriages, & that neither in the Town nor Fort was there a supply of 20 rounds of either Powder or Ball.' It is of course impossible to know whether or not the French knew exactly what the Bishop was up to, and deliberately fed him misleading information in the best tradition of the modern spy novel. Whatever the truth, it is safe to say that the Bishop ran very great risks in all these doings.

In that all these actions were intended to lend support – via Hamilton – to the pro-British Queen of Naples, we see how the Bishop's political bearings had swung around towards the end of his life. For a man who had been immersed in the philosophies of Voltaire, Locke and Rousseau (for a churchman fairly scandalous in itself) and who at one time had virtually been inciting the Irish to armed revolution, the change to backing the autocratic Bourbons was significant. Perhaps it was the shock which ran through the

The memorial obelisk in the grounds at Ickworth.

civilised 'free-thinking' world following the bloodshed and near anarchy of the French Revolution that changed his mind. 'They are a band of Monkeys', he wrote at the beginning of 1791, 'who have burst into a shop of old China & are breaking all about them.'

It makes a happier memory to think of the Bishop as a friend to all, as in the early days of his episcopal career, as liberal in his counsel as with his money, sharing both alike to all denominations. In Ireland there is no monument to this extraordinary man apart from the remaining architecture of Downhill, but in England, in the grounds of Ickworth, there is an obelisk erected by his parishioners which bears the words:

> 'His great patronage was uniformly administered upon the purest and Most distinguished principles. Various and important public works were undertaken at his instigation and completed by his munificence; and hostile sects which had long entertained feelings of deep animosity towards each other were gradually softened and reconciled by his influence and example.'

John Hervey = (1) Isabella Carr
1st Earl of Bristol

= (2) Elisabeth Felton

John, Lord Hervey = Mary Lepel
(1696–1743)

George William
2nd Earl of Bristol
(1721–1775)
Lord Lieutenant of Ireland

Lepel

Augustus John
3rd Earl of Bristol
(1724–1779)
Married in 1744
to Elizabeth Chudleigh
who later made bigamous
marriage to Duke of
Kingston

Mary = George Fitzgerald

George Robert
'Fighting'
Fitzgerald

Mary = John
(1753–) *1st Earl Erne*

Elizabeth Caroline

John Augustus = Elizabeth Drummond
Lord Hervey
(1757–1796)

Elizabeth Catherine

The HERVEY Family Tree

The Bishop's arms

Rev. Henry Hervey-Aston

Henrietta Hervey-Aston = James Bruce

Rev. Henry Hervey Bruce (Harry) Becomes the Bishop's heir to Downhill in 1803

Frideswide = Daniel Mussenden

Frederick *4th Earl of Bristol* Bishop of Derry (1730–1803) = Elizabeth Davers

William

Emily

Caroline

Elizabeth (1758–1824) = (1) John Foster

= (2) William Cavendish *5th Duke of Devonshire*

Frederick

Augustus

Vere Foster

Louisa (1767–1821) = Lord Liverpool

Frederick William *5th Earl and 1st Marquess of Bristol* (1769–1859) The present day Bristol family is descended through this line

Mary Hervey

(Lady Erne)

MARY, the Bishop's first child, was born in 1753 probably at Peterborough. Like Elizabeth, the second daughter, she was a formidable correspondent with her father and throughout his life received letters covering a vast range of subjects from gossip and politics to art, architecture, health and the family. In 1775 she became engaged to Lord Erne, and despite the fact that he already had a family of four from his first marriage, ('– this staggers her', wrote the Bishop) they were married in 1776. In the same year, one of Mary's first wifely duties was to travel with her two step-daughters to their school in Brussels; she was accompanied by her mother and father and her younger sister Louisa, all of whom were setting forth on a *Grand Tour.*

In 1778 she and Lord Erne were in Paris, and while there found that she was expecting a baby, although her condition was wrongly diagnosed by the French doctors who advised warm baths and thus earned the criticism of incompetence from Mary's mother. Mary returned to England and the child was born at Bury in 1779. The Bishop was delighted at the prospect of becoming a grandfather: 'Isn't Mary a sweet creature to be at last multiplying herself, & providing comforts for her old age and mine?' he wrote, going on to envisage Downhill full of the extended family and thoughts of 'building barracks for the children'.

However the marriage was not to last; by 1781, Mary was at Ickworth and being described as 'grown *languissante*'. Even three years previously there had been an inkling that Lord Erne was not proving to be a model husband: writing about Mary, the Bishop said 'He tries her to atoms by his silly difficulties, and by his endless irresolution. Great God! how ill she is matched.' By 1782 Mary was living at Bath, sharing her sorrows with her sister Elizabeth who was also in the process of separation from her husband, John Foster. Whereas Elizabeth's career seems to have blossomed after this (see page 112), Mary's continued rather more quietly, living variously on the Continent and in England and often travelling with the Bishop. The

Mary Hervey, Lady Erne

Bishop seems to have helped her financially somewhat more than Elizabeth, but as the younger sister had been taken up by the well-to-do Devonshires, this may have been quite reasonable. She received a modest allowance from him and he attempted vainly to persuade Lord Erne to support her. He also tried to help in other smaller matters, such as paying for her postage and seeing that she had a decent coach to use when in London: in 1792 he writes 'if your husband will not allow you a Coach in London your Father will – and tho' I never was more pinch'd for money, yet I would beg that you would do the thing handsomely. . .'

At about the same time we find Mary being asked by her father to act as an agent for him, in the business of bidding for pictures to be auctioned at Christie's, though without much success. During his liaison with Mrs Mussenden (see page 46) the Bishop admits to having nicknamed her 'Lady Erne the Second', which suggests that he regarded Mary more as a friend and confidante than as just another one of his children.

After the Bishop's death in 1803, Mary seems to have lived mostly in England. Despite his certain affection for her, she received nothing from her father's will – apparently he felt that having once provided a dowry (as with Elizabeth) nothing further was required. It is difficult to know how much time Mary spent at Downhill, though both a bedroom and a dressing room were there designated as 'Lady Erne's'. Nor can we be sure that the spot overlooking Portvantage Glen with the curious structure known as 'Lady Erne's Seat' (see page 55) was indeed a favourite place of hers, though it is pleasant to think so. Mary died in 1842 at Hampton Court.

John Augustus Hervey

JOHN AUGUSTUS was the Bishop's first son and was born in 1757. In 1770 and 1771 he travelled abroad with his father on the *Grand Tour* which took them all over Europe in pursuit of the Bishop's great interest of the moment, geology. The faithful Shanahan was being towed along too, in order to make drawings. Although the boy was only 13 at this time, he had already commenced a career in the navy, and it is at about this time that we see him dressed in midshipman's uniform in the portrait by Hoare at Ickworth. This picture also shows his father and Lord Chatham (the elder Pitt). While in Italy the Bishop fell ill and John had to write his letters for him, both those concerning business and health. A letter from him to the Count de Salis ends, 'Papa would be much obliged to you if you would send him a dozen or 12 good lemons and if you could send him a very good Physician or doctor...' At the same time he was also writing letters which he was at some pains to keep unknown to his father, having got himself and a young friend into a scrape. Apparently while on a shooting party they became involved in an incident in which a shepherd's dog was shot, and young John's great concern was that the man should be paid off without his father finding out about it. This early episode proved to be an augury, although in later life he was less shy about approaching his father for money!

By 1778 we know from a letter of his mother's that 'Jack' as the family called him, was commanding his own ship, the sloop *Viper.* In 1779 he married a Miss Drummond in Quebec, by which time he was the captain of a man o' war and serving in the American War of Independence. The portrait of him in captain's uniform by Gainsborough, now at Ickworth, shows him at about this time. In 1787 he left the navy and began a career as British Envoy in Florence, appointed to the court of Tuscany. Possibly he had left the navy earlier, as it is known that he was in Rome the year before, chasing the Bishop with requests for cash to pay off his debts; the Bishop's method of dealing with this was to move elsewhere if he got wind of a visit, or if cornered, to issue a flat refusal. John Augustus' propensity for scrapes reached a head during his period as a diplomat, so much

The Bishop presenting his son John Augustus to Lord Chatham, a detail from the picture by William Hoare, 1770. (Right) John Augustus Hervey, by Gainsborough, a detail from the portrait at Ickworth

so that he had to be recalled from his post in 1793. Apart from pursuing other women, he managed to compromise his mission by enormous lapses of tact; sometimes the two were combined, as when he managed to have the French Minister dismissed, though the real reason for this intrigue was a squabble for the favours of a lady. The final straw was apparently his insulting beahaviour towards the Tuscan Court – Lady Webster reported him as having called the Grand Duke a fool and his chief minister a knave. The Bishop's youngest son, Frederick, asked for and was granted the unenviable task of travelling to Florence to break the bad news of his recall to his brother. Frederick too was out of favour with his father, and it had been hoped that he might be reconciled with him during this visit – in the event the Bishop held aloof and they remained on bad terms to the end.

John Augustus was lucky to come out of all this with his Government pension intact, but nevertheless decided to return to the navy, 'where, by-the-bye, he is very unpopular', remarked Lady Webster. In 1796 he died at sea from nothing more extreme than a chill. The Bishop was shattered by the news, despite never having really got on very well with his eldest son in life: the news 'of poor Lord Hervey's *decease* has quite *bouleversé* my already shattered frame', he recorded.

John Augustus seems to have been one of the less attractive of the Bishop's children. He gives an impression of a rather proud and short-tempered man, ill adapted to not getting his own way. There is a story, variously reported, of the Bishop turning him out of Downhill, either for being drunk or for being a Tory; if true it could easily have been for both reasons. Perhaps the last word on his character should be that of Lord Holland: 'Lord Hervey's conduct was intemperate, indecorous, and violent in the extreme'.

Elizabeth Hervey, painted by Angelica Kaufmann in 1784.

Elizabeth Christiana Hervey

ELIZABETH was the Bishop's second daughter and was born in May of 1758 – though her father did not become a Bishop until nine years later. In 1776 she married John Foster of Dunleer in Co. Louth. The Fosters were good friends of the Bishop and his wife, and at the time the match was thoroughly approved of, despite being a matter of the heart rather than of arrangement, which was the more customary thing in such circumstances. No doubt Elizabeth's parents were conscious of their own marriage being a love-match too, and of its having suffered initially from parental disapproval. The Bishop wrote that he liked the young man and thought him 'peculiarly suited to her'. In family correspondence he was jocularly referred to as 'little slimness', 'Monsieur le Sage' or, more frequently, 'little f' (his father of course being 'big F'.) Young John Foster was a member of the Irish House of Commons, and all the prospects looked good.

However it was not to be. By the time Elizabeth was expecting her second child, husband and wife were very much at loggerheads. The family gathered at Ickworth Lodge at the Bishop's instigation in order to try to effect a reconciliation, with Lady Hervey as the arbitrator, but it was to no avail. 'I do not think there is a ray of comfort or hope in it,' she wrote, and of Foster had a rather changed opinion: 'affection [sic], vanity and avarice being all gratified'. Mrs Dillon, a young cousin, visited Ickworth at this time and wrote about Elizabeth that she is 'in the most terrible situation. Her odious husband will settle so little on her that she must be dependent on her father, which is always an unpleasant thing. Her children . . . are to be taken from her.' In fact she did lose the children, and the separation proved to be permanent.

It seems that the pair were completely unsuited temperamentally. Foster emerges as a petulant and inconstant character: 'more absurd & inconsistant that it is possible to express . . . a ship totally without ballast, blown about by every gust of passion, a very tiring companion and unsatisfactory friend,' his mother- in-law wrote, 'how could I be so mistaken in him?' As for Elizabeth, who by all accounts was very beautiful and vivacious, we have a hint of the coming break-up in another of her mother's letters in which she mentions a dissatisfaction with the home and society of Co. Louth; 'I fear she hankers still after a more *brilliant one.*'

Throughout the rupture and afterwards, the Bishop seems to have behaved very coolly towards his daughter. Having been keen that she should stay with Foster even after it was quite obvious that they were quite irreconcilable, he merely sent her £100 as though that would solve all problems; an action many, but most noticably his great enemy Horace Walpole, thought remarkably callous.

However it was at this stage, in 1782, that Elizabeth's life took a new and remarkable course. Georgiana, Duchess of Devonshire, suggested that Elizabeth should become the companion for an illegitimate child (Miss 'W') of the Duke's, and to receive an annuity of £300. Elizabeth took the opportunity thus offered and went on to become not only a dear and intimate friend of the Duchess but also of the Duke. She flourished in the brilliant atmosphere of the Devonshire's house, and the three of them lived and travelled together with a closeness which, in the late eighteenth century, was regarded as scandalous but was none the less tolerated. Public morality was to become rather more severe about such matters in the succeeding century. To begin with Elizabeth was to look after her charge in a villa in Nice, but after a short time she was to be found travelling Europe with her two friends and charming all their wide circle of acquaintances. In 1787 she met Edward Gibbon in Lausanne; possibly in a state of mild euphoria at having just completed his great *Decline and Fall of the Roman Empire*, he offered to marry her. Although the offer was declined, Gibbon remained captivated, referring to 'Bess' as 'this bewitching animal' for whom 'the wisest man . . . would throw away two or three worlds if he had them'. For a man not usually celebrated for passionate outbursts, this testifies to the remarkable attraction Elizabeth exercised. Among Elizabeth's other gifts was an artistic one. She illustrated Georgiana's poetry, and like her father was to become the friend and patron of many contemporary artists.

Strangely her relationship with her father seems to have remained much the same despite this curious turn of fate; at least from the Bishop's point of view. They had always corresponded fairly voluminously and this certainly was to continue – at least, Elizabeth certainly received many letters from her father; her own

The Duchess of Devonshire

replies have not survived. The traffic of letters was very much one way over the issue of his youngest son's marriage (see page 126). The Bishop's great scheme in 1796 was to marry off young Frederick into the Royal Family of Prussia, and it appears that Elizabeth was to be appointed broker whether she liked it or no. Writing from Germany, he bombarded his poor daughter with demands and entreaties to encourage the match, none of which Elizabeth seems to have answered, or so we must assume as the final letters on the subject become increasingly exasperated: 'You nasty little Imp of Silence!' he calls her in one letter, and asks 'Are you alive or dead, or are you on a journey?' in another. In the event Frederick married the lady of his choice as Elizabeth probably knew he would.

Family matters were not the only topic of correspondence. The Bishop perhaps realised that his daughter's position in the Devonshire household could be very influential, and so he quite frequently aired his political ideas – at length – in the hopes that these ideas might thus gain a wider audience. Both his grand schemes for the splitting up of Holland and for the division of France were promoted in this manner. These letters are similar in tone to those he was wont to write her before the separation on such subjects as the Catholics in Ireland. They often suggest that the Bishop used her as a sort of sounding board for his ideas. Not all the Bishop's letters were like this; in 1798 he was writing to her in the hopes that, with her familiarity with diplomats, nobility and members of the governments, she would help in the matter of regaining all his art treasures which had been seized in Rome by the French (see page 83).

We can gain some idea of the circles in which Elizabeth moved with the Devonshire *ménage à trois* by the diversity of her friends and correspondents, numbered among whom were the great Whig orator Charles James Fox, the playwright Sheridan, the Duke of Wellington, Lady Holland, the artists Canova and Thorwaldson, Lord Byron and even the Prince Regent. In 1806 the Duchess of Devonshire died, and Elizabeth was deeply affected by the loss: to her son Augustus she wrote, 'who ever filled such a space as she did in society? To whom was she as she was to me?' In 1809 she became the Duke's wife, thus making acceptable to the world at large a relationship which had existed for the previous 27 years. She had secretly borne the Duke a child in 1785, a daughter who was brought up as Caroline 'St Jules', and also a son, William 'Clifford', in 1788. When the Duke himself died in 1811 Elizabeth then moved to live in Rome and kept a salon there in every way as brilliant as that of the Devonshires. An observer wrote that one went to her 'conversaziones as to a great exchange to see who is in Rome, and to meet what is called the world.' At this latter end of her life she devoted much time to the patronage of the arts and also to what we would now call archaeology, spending quite a deal of money on the excavation of the Forum. In 1816 we find her writing to her son Augustus: 'I have begun a little excavation in the Foro Romano, and they found a little cup or calice [sic]. In digging close to the single Pillar, they found it to be a column to Phocas. I am having the Cup cleaned a little and put together.'

There can be no doubt that Elizabeth was a fascinating, talented and very handsome woman. Her portrait was painted by Reynolds, Gainsborough and Lawrence, though perhaps the finest picture of her is that by Angelica Kauffmann which can be seen today at Ickworth. On looking at this charming portrait it is not difficult to understand Gibbon's enthusiasm, surely shared by countless others: 'if she chose to beckon the Lord Chancellor from his woolsack in full sight of the world, he could not resist obedience!' She died in 1824, and her body was brought back from Rome to be buried beside the Duke and his first Duchess in the Cavendish family vault in Derby .

John Thomas Foster

ELIZABETH'S FIRST HUSBAND was the son of Dr Thomas Foster who was the rector of Dunleer in Co. Louth. At the time of their marriage, he was the member for Ennis in the Irish Parliament, which the Bishop saw as an ideal employment for a son-in-law because it would keep him in touch with the pulse of Irish politics, especially on the 'Catholic Question', even when he was abroad. In a letter from the Bishop to Elizabeth dated from the autumn of 1778 he asks her to persuade her husband to send 'a list of the speakers in our house on the Popish bill, and the sum of the argument against us; that I wish also to know if the bill to tolerate their religion is to take place, without which I do not know how the multitiude are benefitted.'

Unfortunately the marriage only lasted until 1780, so the Bishop can not have made very much use of Foster. However, after the break-up, Foster took custody of his two young sons, Frederick George and Augustus. In 1784 the Bishop's wife wrote to her daughter with news of her lost family (Foster's father had just died) saying 'I know you will be very uneasy about the poor boys' and adding that there was not much hope of the Bishop's settling anything with Foster: 'I wrote to him when he was in Dublin to beg he would get your settlement registered, and his answer was that he would have nothing more to do with Mr F.' Mr F. seems to have been more attached to his children than to his wife, at least to judge from another letter to Elizabeth from her mother in 1792: '. . . both are very fine boys. Frederick is very sentimental, sedate and sensible . . . the youngest seems arch, lively, and sensible, and I think has much of Lord Bristol in him, and they are very good-natured boys, and always seem happy to see us; indeed, the father seems very fond of them both, and takes great care of them.'

Frederick Foster 1777–

Frederick, Elizabeth and Foster's first son, took the title Oriel, like his father's cousin, and is commemorated by a statue at Ardee, between Drogheda and Dundalk, put up at the expense of 'his tenantry'.

Augustus Foster 1780–1848

Augustus was the second son of Elizabeth and Foster. He was educated at Oxford, entered the army for a period and then went into the diplomatic service. He acted as ambassador to the United States of America but was not greatly effectual in preventing the hostilities which broke out between England and that nation in 1812. He served then in Denmark and finally at the court of the King of Sardinia until retirement in 1840. He was made a baronet in his own right in 1831, and took the title from his home at Glyde Court in Co. Louth. He died in 1848, apparently by suicide, leaving his wife Albinia and three sons.

Vere Foster 1819–1900

Vere Foster was one of Augustus's sons. He was born in Copenhagen when his father was in the diplomatic mission there. He began life in the foreign service too, and served in Argentina until his father's death. On returning to Ireland, then in the grip of 'the great hunger', he was so appalled at the condition of the people and especially of those who attempted to emigrate, that he devoted the rest of his life and all of his own fortune to philanthropy.

Vere Foster

Not only did he provide money to help would-be emigrants but was also largely instrumental in pushing through the legislation to improve and control the conditions of passage on the notorious 'coffin ships'. Having made the voyage himself – and survived it – he was able to argue from experience. Less spectacular but longer lasting was the effect that he had on the problems of education in Ireland; he donated sums of money for the improvement of over 2,000 National schools right across the country and was a main force in the founding of the Irish National Teachers organisation. He is perhaps most generally remembered for the famous Vere Foster copybooks which he devised and had printed at his own expense, and which set the pattern for the teaching of handwriting for years to come.

John Foster, Baron Oriel, 1740–1828

John Foster was first cousin to Elizabeth's husband, and was an important figure in Irish politics. He was the last Speaker in the Irish House of Commons, and though very much a supporter of the ascendancy, bitterly opposed the Act of Union in 1800, being one of the very few parliamentarians whose vote could not be bought; the historian Lecky wrote that there was 'clearly no chance of bribing him into acquiescence by honours or money.' Foster's disillusionment over the corruption of this manoeuvre was such that he refused to surrender either the mace or the Speaker's chair.

Foster retired to his home at Oriel Temple, in Collon Co. Louth, and devoted himself to extending and developing his gardens. He is credited with starting one of the first nurseries for seedlings and his collection formed much of the beginnings of the Botanical Gardens at Glasnevin. A contemporary writer said of Oriel: 'In this seminary I beheld the greatest variety of shrubs, evergreen and deciduous forest trees I have ever seen.' He was created Baron Oriel in 1821.

Louisa Hervey

(Lady Liverpool)

LOUISA was the Bishop's third daughter and was born in 1767. At the tender age of ten she accompanied her father on one of his exhausting European tours, stopping first in Paris with Lady Erne, and then continuing on to Brussels and Liège, where the party were to leave Lady Erne's stepdaughters at a convent for their education, and where Louisa too would have been ready to stay, 'being quite at ease among the Nuns, and singing both English and French to them', as her mother wrote. The faithful Bitio was also with the party, but he was despatched early on to draw volcanoes in the Auvergne (see page 92) while the rest travelled on to Pyrmont, Mayence, Mannheim, Verona and finally Rome, where they stayed at Castle Gandolfo.

Louisa was greatly admired in Rome; her mother wrote that 'Louisa is not really spoilt by . . . the admiration of all the Artists who tease one to death to let them copy her dear face.' However it was here that the whole household fell victim to influenza, which in those days could be fatal. The Bishop, writing in 1778 to his friend Sir William Hamilton, recounts that Louisa 'is still faintly recovering after a medical sentence pronounced on her that she had but a quarter of an hour to live.' There can be no doubt that she was very ill indeed, and her mother too, at one stage, believed that she would die: 'in the midst of her illness she called out suddenly – Oh Mama I am going to be very happy – I own I thought so; for I expected death to deliver her.' However she did recover and a little concert was held to celebrate, with words and music specially composed for the occasion, following which the family moved on to Naples. Then in 1779 they set off for home again, via Lausanne, where again she was greatly admired: 'The beauty of her person . . . the grace of her singing . . . she had charmed the whole world here' as one commentator put it, and all this in a young lady not yet twelve.

Back in England, staying at Ickworth, Lady Hervey painted an idyllic picture of the relationship between herself and her daughter; Louisa, aged twelve, playing out of doors on a frosty May Day morning from about 5am had planted a maypole and crowned it with early flowers. Her mama admired it but reproved her for being 'so much out of rule without leave' and she was sent in. Then mother relented and decorated the maypole herself with 'a beautiful knot of magnificent ribband' and a set of no doubt moralistic verses of her own composition (a dialogue between pleasure and memory) and then the girl was allowed out again. It had its 'effect in a moment & she ran into my room immediately & in the prettiest manner & with all ye sensibility of my *dearest Mary* thanked me for my addition to her may-pole but *more* for the paper she found on it.'

Louisa was not to prove quite so charming or grateful over the matter of a new dress which her father had sent her; in 1787 he writes from Downhill to his daughter Mary 'Louisa has *sold* the beautiful gown I gave her, because the shape was not *fashionable*, and I have redeem'd it & paid her the price.' It should be remembered that at this time Louisa was living with her mother at Ickworth and that the parents had more or less separated some four years previously; possibly the youngest daughter's behaviour in this matter had been influenced by her mother. Life at Ickworth was evidently dull, especially as they could not come to London as the Bishop had let the house in St James's Square, which of course rather frustrated Louisa's 'coming out'. However they did come to London, in opposition to the Bishop's wishes, in order to consult doctors following some sort of nervous breakdown. The tedium of Ickworth (where even Mama was inclined to censor her reading) was then broken by the same doctors' prescription of 'moderate and cheerful amusements'.

The Bishop did appear to still care for his youngest daughter – perhaps even more than for his abandoned wife – for in 1792, writing to Lady Erne, we find him mentioning a small sum of money sent with the aim of providing 'sweet Louisa her opera ticket'. In 1795 Louisa was married to Robert Banks Jenkinson, who in 1796 became Lord Hawkesbury when his father was made Earl of Liverpool. The Bishop corresponded with the father, who was then Secretary of State, over the sequestration of his art treasures by the French, even offering a picture, 'a Gem of Guercino's', by way of encouraging governmental action over their return. Whether this inducement, or indeed any of the others, including a Raphael and a Salvator Rosa (the last sent c/o Louisa) ever actually changed hands is not known, but the great bulk of his collection was never ultimately returned (see page 83). His son Frederick was Under Secretary in the same office

Louisa Hervey, an engraving after Romney's portrait.

but it seems to have made no difference. In course of time Louisa's husband became the second Lord Liverpool and, in 1812, Prime Minister; 'one of England's dullest' according to one biographer. Louisa may have had some of this rubbed off on her; 'her extreme prudery . . . an odd & questionable aspect for a Hervey' was noted by Lady Bessborough.

Louisa's health does not seem to have improved greatly under the various stresses of being a cabinet minister's wife. She was said to be prone to hysterics, and was reported to have fainted on hearing the news of the Cato Street conspirancy. By the year 1802 she was taking what she described as 'poppies' – possible laudanum – to help her sleep. However she certainly took her duties seriously, being required to attend the embarcation of Louis XVIII at Dover in 1814, when he returned to Francc to reclaim the throne; and to entertain the politicians and diplomats of her husband's circle at Coombe

House, their home near Richmond. Mme de Stael also visited there (having first had considerable difficulty finding the place).

The couple did not have any children, though it might be inferred that Louisa would have liked a family; a contemporary spoke of 'Lady Hawkesbury's children that never came to maturity and have great doubts of whether they ever existed'. She involved herself in good works and was generally credited with piety. When she died, on 12 June 1821, Lord Liverpool had the following inscription placed on the statue of her by Chantrey:

> 'She visited the fatherless, and widows in their affliction.
> And kept herself unspotted from the world.'

This monument to her is presently in the parish church of All Saints, Kingston-upon-Thames. She also sat to Nollekens for a portrait bust about the year 1801, but one of the most charming representations of her is the portrait by Romney, which can be seen today in the drawing room at Ickworth. In this she is shown as a young woman with a rather dreamy expression, leaning on her harp (could O'Hempsey's harp, see page 183, have been used as the 'prop'?) This probably shows her as she would have appeared at the time of her marriage.

Louisa, from Chantrey's monument in Kingston church, London.

Lord Liverpool

LORD LIVERPOOL is often only remembered as being a rather colourless politician at the time of the Napoleonic Wars; however he must have been an extremely able one, if only on the evidence of his having held the post of prime minister continuously for longer – 15 years – than any other in the nineteenth century, and at a time when the government was formed largely by coalition.

He was born Robert Banks Jenkinson in 1770 and was educated at Charterhouse and Christchurch, Oxford. At the age of 19 he witnessed the fall of the Bastille, a wholly suitable omen for a budding Whig. He held a parliamentary seat for Appleby and then Rye, and was appointed speaker in Pitt's government of 1791. In 1793 he met Louisa, the Bishop's youngest daughter, and they fell in love, becoming engaged in 1794. They had to wait until the next year to marry because of his father witholding his consent, Robert being too young (at 24) in his opinion, and only giving way after gentle pressure from Pitt and, it is said, the king. The couple were married in Wimbledon.

Louisa and Robert lived variously at Coombe House which was near Richmond Park in London, and at Walmer Castle, which was a perquisite attached to the post of Lord Warden of the Cinque Ports. The king himself visited Coombe in June of 1805, and it seems to have been the main house for the Liverpools; or at least sufficiently important to them to have John Soane – who had once worked for the Bishop – to design improvements for it. The family seat was at Hawkesbury in the Cotswolds and thus too far from Robert's work, and Walmer, being an official residence was perhaps less comfortable – although it was lent on occasion to Louisa's sister Elizabeth.

Robert, who held the title of Lord Hawkesbury from 1796, became the 2nd Earl of Liverpool on his father's death; Louisa thus became Lady Liverpool. When Lord Liverpool became Prime Minister in 1812 it was the culmination of a series of increasingly important appointments: Master of the Royal Mint, Secretary of State, Secretary for War, Secretary for the Colonies. As Prime Minister he exercised what have been described as 'solid but not shining talents' through one after another constitutional crisis in the wake of the war

Lord Liverpool, detail from the portrait by Thomas Lawrence, 1804.

with France. The country was suffering an economic depression after the years of struggle, added to which a series of poor harvests led to public insurrections which in turn required more repressive and unpopular measures. The Peterloo massacre in 1819 was the most spectacular of these riots, and Liverpool's government went so far as to suspend *Habeas Corpus*. The king's notorious divorce case in 1820 again rocked the cabinet, but Liverpool somehow managed to hang on. On top of all this, trouble erupted in Ireland in 1822 and in 1825 there was a disastrous failure of the English banking system. It was not an easy time to be Prime Minister. However Liverpool managed to keep his ministry together up until 1826 when a general election returned him to power; but then illness overtook him in the following year, forcing his retirement, and ultimately his death.

Louisa had died in June of 1821, and Liverpool, a man easily given to tears according to contemporaries, was devastated. Her will required that her husband should lay her in her coffin with his own hands; understandably this was almost beyond his powers. Notwithstanding his deep attachment to Louisa (he kept the statue of her which he had commissioned from Chantrey in the house at Coombe until the end of his life), he married again in 1822, a Miss Chester. There were no children from either marriage.

Lord Liverpool seems to have been possessed of a very temporising nature, noted for his 'tact, practicality, & good temper'. He deserves a better memory perhaps from posterity for his farsighted support of the concept of National Museums, being one of the first Trustees of the National Gallery and also of the British Museum. He had his own portrait painted, twice by Hoppner and three times by Lawrence; one of the latter is at Ickworth, as is a bust by Nollekens.

Frederick William Hervey

(Fifth Earl of Bristol)

FREDERICK was the Bishop's fifth child and was born in 1769. In 1775 a letter of the Bishop's discusses the qualities required in a tutor for the boy, 'I could wish for a mathematical and physical turn in my tutor . . . I could wish also for some knowledge in the languages, and, above all, a perfect gentleness of temper'. Whatever the tutor he got, he certainly did very well at university, passing all his examinations with 'wonderful credit and *éclat*' and being 'declared first of his year in every subject.' By the age of fifteen he had been made the nominal colonel of the Tyrone Battalion of the Volunteers and had attended their reviews with his father. A tailor's bill of 1785 lists clothes made for 'Master Harvey', including two suits of 'Regimentils'. The Dublin Evening Post described him as 'a really fine-spirited young fellow and as warm a friend to this country as his father.' The following year he went with the Bishop and his retinue ('the clods I bring with me') to Lyons and thence to Rome.

By 1787 however, the relationship between father and son, which had seemed initially to have gone very well, began to disintegrate. All the causes of the rupture are not known, but part of the problem may well have been Frederick's refusal, backed by his mother, to be sent to the Low Countries for yet more education. The Bishop had finally fallen out with his wife some five years previously. Howsoever it was, the young man was referred to as 'my undutiful and ungrateful son' in the will of 1791 and left with the comparatively small sum of £1,000.

In 1793 Frederick travelled to Florence to deliver to his elder brother the unhappy news of his dismissal from the post of Minister there (see page 108). From this we may guess that he was in the diplomatic service at the time, and that he must have done well in this career as later, in the early years of the nineteenth century, he held the position of Under Secretary for Foreign Affairs. In 1796 John Augustus died and Frederick therefore became Lord Hervey and indeed heir apparent to his father's title.

Frederick, 1st Marquess of Bristol, by Hoppner.
Ickworth in the lower left background.

It was in this same year that the Bishop began working in earnest on his scheme to marry Frederick off to the daughter of his great friend the Countess von Lichtenau. This latest 'luminous idea' was pressed with great assiduity by the Bishop who could see nothing but advantages in the match to everyone concerned, not excluding himself. The lady in question, the Countess Mariana, would bring '£5,000 a year, *besides* a principality in Germany, an English Dukedom for Frederick or me, . . . a perpetual relationship with both the Princess of Wales. . .' and much more. The reality of all this was that the Bishop's intention was to ally his family with that of the royal house of Prussia: the Countess Mariana was in fact the daughter –

albeit illegitimate – of the King of Prussia and of the Countess von Lichtenau, his mistress of some years before, when she was plain Madame Ritz. Frederick was urged to come to Pyrmont to meet his intended, his sisters were urged to persuade him so to do, the Countess was instructed to have a portrait done of her daughter, and the king himself prevailed upon to issue the relevant passports.

Alas, Frederick's character was the equal to that of his father and he had already determined to take a wife of his own choosing. This was doubly galling for his father because the lady of his choice was Elizabeth Upton, sister to Lord Templeton who had also had an affair with his new friend the Countess von Lichtenau before (and had once boxed her ears) – not a family with whom the Bishop was likely to be on good terms. Added to which she was considerably under-funded: in one of his concluding – and despairing – letters on the subject to his daughter Elizabeth, the Bishop drew up the matter like a bill of accounts: on the one side (his), '£5,000 a year down. £5,000 a year in reversion. An English Dukedom. Royal connexion. Embassy to Berlin or Munich.'; while on the other side (Frederick's), 'No fortune. Wife and children beggars for want of settlement. No connexion.' In 1797 Frederick married Miss Upton and, no doubt, was happy.

We do not know for certain if father and son were reconciled after this, although the Bishop's biographer, Childe Pemberton, suggests that they were, without giving more details. Towards the end of his life, the Bishop refers to his son as 'dear Lord Hervey', which lends weight to the idea. When the Bishop died in 1803 Frederick became the 5th Earl of Bristol and inherited all the English property, which of course included the incomplete house at Ickworth. In 1826 he became the first Marquess of Bristol and lived on to the grand age of 90. The Bristol title today is descended from this branch of the Bishop's family.

Frederick seems to have been the most likeable of the Bishop's two sons, having inherited much of his mother's common sense. Two portraits of him, one by Hoppner and a later one by Lawrence can be seen today at Ickworth.

George William Hervey

(Second Earl of Bristol)

GEORGE WILLIAM HERVEY, the first son of John Lord Hervey and grandson of the 1st Earl of Bristol, was born in 1721. All accounts suggest that he never enjoyed good health but nevertheless followed his father's political footsteps as a prominent Whig. He took the title of Baron Hervey of Ickworth on the death of his father in 1743, and appears to have spent quite a large part of his early life between Ickworth and London seeking preferment both for himself and for his three younger brothers. The breakthrough in his fortunes came after the death of his grandfather in 1751 and his subsequent elevation to the title of 2nd Earl of Bristol. More importantly he was heir to the old Earl's fortune and property. (Bypassing one's immediate heirs seems to have been a characteristic of the Herveys.) In the same year he turned down the offer of the post of Lord of the Bedchamber to the young Prince of Wales, possibly in hopes of a better position in a warmer climate as the Envoy to Portugal or even Spain. This would indicate either good sense – his brother Augustus reported that George was making no progress at Court; 'the King frequently rumped him' (turned his back on him) – or a showing of the arrogance often attributed to him.

His first diplomatic post came in 1775 when he became the British Minister to the King of Sardinia at Turin; this position having been obtained for him through the influence of the Duke of Newcastle who in return had the use of his proxy vote in the House of Lords – such were the politics of the time. (It was probably from this period that the curious acquisition of portraits of the Sardinian Royal Family came to Ickworth.) William Cole wrote:

> 'He was a very worthy nobleman and is now Ambassador at the Court in Turin. His Lordship is well versed in English history, antiquities, and heraldry, and is besides a very accomplished nobleman in every other respect, but of a most delicate and tender constitution, which made him desirous of going into warmer climes.'

George Hervey, in his ducal robes, by Zoffany, *c.*1759.

The torso of George's statue from the Mausoleum, by van Nost.

The next post was the more important one of Ambassador to the Court of Spain in 1755. His naval brother Augustus was serving in the Mediterranean at this time and in 1758 sailed him from Genoa to Alicante on board HMS *Monmouth*, remarking in his journal, apparently without any irony, 'I was surprised my brother was so little sick.' Augustus also reported a significant detail of George's character when he described the formalities of disembarcation at Alicante;

after the usual firing of salutes and flag hoisting, George found that the Spanish Customs authorities had taped and sealed his baggage, 'on which he took out his sisars and cut before their faces before he stepped into the coach.'

The most significant appointment for George, now Lord Bristol, came in 1766 with the return of Pitt to political power in England, who gave him the Lord Lieutenancy of Ireland. It was generally supposed that George would be the right man to implement some administration reforms including, it was hinted, some measure of Catholic relief. Not everyone was convinced; Horace Walpole said of him that 'his stately manners and delicate form were ill-adapted to please so rude and turbulent people as the Irish.' (Walpole had also once described him as 'a very Spaniard in formality and pride.') However Pitt was at this time holding together a very shaky coalition and was in poor health, which apparently made it so difficult for Lord Bristol that he felt he had to resign after only one year in office. It was a busy year all the same, as during the time he managed to promote his younger brother Frederick first of all to the post of chaplain to the king and then to the Bishopric of Cloyne, with the ultimate aim of that of Derry. The fact that Lord Bristol never set foot in Ireland and was no longer Lord Lieutenant when Derry became vacant in 1768 seems not to have affected his influence with the king over the appointment. The king rather regretted it later.

George, Lord Bristol, died of the 'gout' on the 18th of March 1775 at Bath. Walpole said that this complaint (whatever it was) was hereditary and that he used to starve himself to stave off the symptoms. Certainly he does not look particularly robust in the best picture we have of him, by Zoffany, now at Ickworth. The death of George, who had never married and had no heir of his own, meant that the earldom passed to the next brother Augustus; he was by now a Vice-Admiral but, because of his ill advised marriage to the bigamous Elizabeth Chudleigh, had no legitimate heir and this put the Bishop in the position of next in line for the Bristol title. Truly, he had much to thank George for, and the Mausoleum (see page 33) which he had erected at Downhill with its statue by van Nost, was a lasting witness of his gratitude.

Augustus John Hervey

(Third Earl of Bristol)

AUGUSTUS HERVEY DESERVES a place in this survey on his own account, quite apart from his being the instrument of his younger brother's final step on fortune's ladder to the Bristol title, a step which – had it been in his power – he would have almost certainly tried to prevent.

Augustus' career was in the navy, and the fact of his rising to the rank of Vice-Admiral in the service was a testament to his abilities rather than the more normal method of political preferment, since for most of his life he was in opposition to the prevailing faction of the government. He first went to sea at the age of 11 as 'Captain's Servant', otherwise a cadet, on his uncle William Hervey's ship the *Pembroke*, mostly in the West Indies. The Royal Navy of this time was – to put it at its mildest – a rough discipline, so the circumstance of uncle William having 'the misfortune of being dismissed the service' on the grounds of excessive brutality by a court-martial in 1742, suggests that Augustus's early years at sea probably hardened him to the naval life fairly rapidly. He next served as lieutenant of the *Sutherland* under Captain Byng, and formed a lasting friendship with him from that time. Promotion came slowly and he did not get his own command, the sloop *Porcupine* until 1746, but was then quite quickly promoted to the much larger *Princessa* of 74 guns; rather too large by his own admission, he would have preferred a smaller, faster vessel which might have afforded better chances of taking prizes while 'cruising'.

For the ensuing ten years Augustus spent most of his time cruising in the 'straits', that is, in the Mediterranean between the Straits of Gibraltar and Italy, engaged in harrying the French and Spanish (this is the period of the War of Jenkin's Ear) and carrying out diplomatic missions. When not at sea, he devoted his time to philandering, this occupation being conducted both in the court at Lisbon and latterly at Versailles, and in politicking at home, particularly in his strenuous opposition to the harsh requirements of the Navy Bill of 1749. An incident in 1748 demonstrates his singular personal courage (or lack of imagination): When a merchantman, heavily car-

Augustus John Hervey, painted by Gainsborough, with the naval assault on Havana in the background.

goed with powder, caught fire in the harbour at Leghorn (Livorno) no-one but Hervey would go near her so, in his own words,

> 'I went on board her and cut her cables with my own hand that was fast ashore, and towed her out, having my coat burnt almost all the skirts off. As soon as I had towed her clear, she blew up, and hurt none of our boats, but made a most violent blast.'

Towards the end of this spell Augustus was commanding the 20-gun *Phoenix*, and it was in this vessel that he took part in the battle of Mahon, an attempt to prevent the French from invading Minorca, in 1756. The British fleet, under Byng, failed to disperse the French, partly through the indecisiveness of the admiral, and the garrison on the island fell, thus losing Britain a most important base in the Western Mediterranean. Byng was recalled and made the political scapegoat, court martialled and ultimately shot 'pour encourager les autres' in the ironic words of Voltaire. Augustus defended his friend and patron loyally right up to the very end, giving evidence, mustering support and pamphleteering; he even proposed a last-ditch escape plan.

After the débâcle of Mahon, Augustus got the *Hampton Court* of 64 guns and served under Admiral Hawke in the Mediterranean, mainly involved in keeping the French bottled up there and preventing their ships from sailing to the support of their colonists in America. The most spectacular action from this time was the chase and cutting off of four French ships in what became known as the 'moonlight battle' in March of 1758. Following this, he spent an arduous period in 1759 blockading the French off Brest in the *Monmouth*. He kept his ship at sea for 21 weeks and was so successful in containing the enemy that he gained high praise from the normally very restrained Hawke.To his great chagrin he had to come off the station just before Hawke's victory at Quiberon Bay.

The final part of his seafaring career was in command of the *Dragon* in the West Indies. In 1762 he was in the force which captured Havana from the Spanish, and this was to be the final engagement of his career at sea. The famous Gainsborough portrait of him which hangs at Ickworth shows him in Captain's uniform at the siege of Moro Castle at the harbour at Havana. Thereafter he pursued a land-based occupation, as an active debater in both Houses of Parliament and latterly as a Lord of the Admiralty. He died in 1779.

That the Bristol earldom passed from Augustus to his younger brother – the Bishop – was the direct result of his being embroiled in one of the most notorious bigamy cases of the eighteenth century. As a very young lieutenant he had married in secret a certain Miss Chudleigh, a maid of honour to the Princess of Wales. Miss Chudleigh had no doubt got an eye on the strong possibility of shortly becoming the Duchess of Bristol, since the elder brother George – unmarried and childless – seemed very unlikely to recover from his recurrent ill-health. However George did recover, Augustus went to sea, and his erstwhile bride proceeded to chase after a succession of lovers, most of whom had titles. She appears to have been the classic adventuress, with a certain flair for self-publicity – at the Venetian Ambassador's Ball at Somerset House in 1749 she appeared in the costume of 'Iphigenia for the sacrifice, but so naked the high priest might easily inspect the entrails of the victim. The Maids of Honour (not of maids the strictest) were so offended they would not speak to her'. Fifteen years after the ceremony, she decided to have the details entered in the parish register, as once again it seemed likely that Augustus would succeed to the title; their relationship had cooled very rapidly within the first few months, so this was sheer opportunism. Nevertheless George recovered yet again.

After a further nine years it was Augustus who brought the matter to a head. He was toying with the idea of a new marriage and threatened a divorce action on the grounds of her adultery; but in the end she bought his silence with a sum rumoured to have been enormous, and left an ecclesiastical court with a declaration that he could not maintain that she had ever been his wife. Then almost immediately she married the Duke of Kingston in 1769. He lasted only four years and died leaving most of his estates to his widow, passing over some disgruntled nephews in the process. One of the nephews found out about her original marriage to Augustus, produced the parish register plus one of the witnesses and had her brought to court on a charge of bigamy. There was then a scandal, she was found guilty, fined and subsequently escaped to the Continent.

Where all these matrimonial shenanigans left the Bristol title was simple, if rather painful, for Augustus and rather fortunate for his younger brother Frederick: since Miss Chudleigh was indeed married to Augustus (who by this time *was* the 3rd Earl) but also well and truly estranged, it was impossible for him to have a legitimate heir. Thus was the title to pass to the Bishop.

This is not to say of course that Augustus had no children – indeed Miss Chudleigh herself had borne him a child which did not survive – for even if half of the liaisons mentioned in his private 'Journal' had been fruitful the Continent would have been as prolific with Herveys as it was with Bristol hotels. The amorous adventures so candidly mentioned in his journal were so numerous that they earned him the nickname 'the English Casanova', though the editor of those memoirs points out that though Casanova is well known to have invented quite a few of his conquests, Augustus' accounts – never having been intended for publication – are disarmingly honest.

Augustus' tastes ranged from servant girls to duchesses and princesses. He was apparently quite capable of running great risks in avoiding husbands of various of the attached noble ladies, hiding in beds, behind curtains, creeping in and out via stables and so on. This was the procedure with two of his most celebrated loves, Madame de Caze in Paris and Madame Brignole-Sale in Genoa; however it was another lady who herself took the initiative in one of his most spectacular exploits – this was the Duchess of Cadaval who, in 1753, had him kidnapped in Lisbon and contrived to remain incognito throughout their several assignations. On the first of these occasions Augustus was justifiably most unsure of what was going to happen, but had the presence of mind to put his pistols under the pillow.

It may have been this free and easy mode of life which caused the disaffection between him and his younger brother. It has been said that at the time of Augustus's wishing to remarry in 1768, the Bishop was quite prepared to bring to light the damning information of the Chudleigh affair itself, though probably less from a sense of moral duty than a desire to keep himself in the running for an earldom. Augustus's 'Journal' once records the chance discovery of some marginal notes made by brother Frederick in a book he had been reading which evidently confirmed what Augustus thought of him, 'fixed me with regard to him', but he irritatingly fails to elaborate on the matter.

The Barnards

THE BARNARD FAMILY was closely connected with the Bishop ever since he succeeded Dr William Barnard as the Bishop of Derry in 1786. William Barnard's son, the Rev. Dr Henry was rector of Maghera, and the friendship between the two families was confirmed when his daughter Letitia married the Bishop's protegé, Harry Bruce, in 1786. How close they all were may be judged from the fact that they were all together at Bath the previous year, the Bishop referring to them as 'the Dear Barnards' and 'the Dear Friendly Family with whom I entirely live, nine hours of the twenty four only excepted'. On that occasion Letitia seems to have been rather ill, and the Bishop recorded that it was probably the fault of the doctors who had recommended the waters of Bath which had 'inflam'd her blood' instead of those of Tunbridge which would have 'brac'd her nerves'. Ill health apparently prevented them all from travelling on to Italy in company with the Bishop.

The Barnards were also neighbours of the Bishop, living in Banbrook House, or Bann Lodge, and once called Barnard's Lodge. The house which originally dates from 1691, was added to by the Bishop who rented it to the Barnards. When all the Irish property passed to Harry Bruce by the terms of the Bishop's will, the house went with it.

Thomas Barnard was rector of Dunboe between 1761 and 1769; he was also Archdeacon of Derry, because at this time the two appointments went together automatically. He was married twice, and his second wife Sarah was buried in the old Dunboe churchyard.

George Robert Fitzgerald

('Fighting Fitzgerald')

GEORGE ROBERT FITZGERALD was the eldest son of the Bishop's sister Lady Mary and a wealthy gentleman from Mayo. His mother and father parted company early on and young George was brought up in England by his mother. Initially he seems to have been the model of good breeding, well-travelled and well-mannered enough to have been presented at the French Court, literary, and capable of producing both reasonable poetry and prose. However he was then to develop into an extraordinarily wild and lawless character. The Bishop who perhaps saw more of the former side of his nature than the latter, apparently had a great deal of affection for him, reaching a high point during the Volunteer Convention in Dublin in 1783.

During that time Fitzgerald acted as the Bishop's *aide de camp*, providing the extravagent military escort that the Bishop required then for his public appearances (see page 98), and having him as a house guest in his establishment in Merrion Square. It is almost inconceivable that his uncle (who, incidentally, favoured him with a 'gift' of £1,000 for these services) could possibly have been ignorant of the fact that earlier in the same year he had been serving a prison sentence. His trial and commitment had been brought about in the first place for the holding as hostage of his father with whom he was constantly quarrelling – in one version, kidnapping him in a coach with a bear (albeit muzzled) for company – the charges having been instigated by a younger brother. It seems that many other charges *could* have been brought, including intimidation and aggravated murder, but it was difficult to make such indictments hold against a man who was either admired or feared by all in the surrounding county. Similarly, it was very difficult to arrest him, given that his house was garrisoned with two to three hundred 'ruffians' forming a kind of private army, and was defended with cannon: to keep him imprisoned was no easier. Legend has it that he enjoyed riding to hounds by torchlight in the hours of darkness; if true it must have been as much for the pleasure of the chase as for the fun of striking terror

Lady Mary Fitzgerald, the Bishop's sister, and mother of the notorious 'fighting' Fitzgerald.

into the hearts of what must have been at the least a rather nervous tenantry. What certainly was true was his reputation as a quickly roused duellist and, if only because of his success in some 26 credited encounters, a very accurate shot.

Such then was the Bishop's intimate in these Convention years. He was even granted the freedom of the City of Londonderry, largely through his uncle's influence. On the other hand, the contemporary rumours that his uncle had ordained him and obtained for him secular 'preferments' worth £2,000 per annum were false. It seems strange that only two years later the Bishop's favour was to be of no use to him when the law finally caught up with him, a £3,000 bounty on his head. In 1786, following more mayhem and murder, Fitzgerald was arrested, tried and executed in his home town of Castlebar. Even then there were difficulties, the hangman's rope breaking on the first attempt. The Bishop was far away in Italy by this time, and was deeply shaken when he eventually received the news in Florence.

'Fighting' Fitzgerald seems to have been one of those outrageous picaresque characters more suited to a Hollywood film script than to real episodes in Irish history, and to have been surrounded with the same kind of glamour as a successful modern gangster.

Rev. Henry Hervey-Aston

James Bruce = Henrietta Hervey-Aston

Rev. Sir Henry Hervey Aston Bruce = Letitia Barnard
1st Baronet Downhill
(1752–1822)

Frederick Hervey

Sir James Robertson Bruce = Ellen Hesketh
2nd Baronet Downhill
(1788–1836)

Sir Henry Hervey Bruce = Marianne Margaret Clifton
3rd Baronet Downhill
(1820–1907)

James Andrew

Sir Hervey Juckes Lloyd Bruce = Ellen Maud Ricardo
4th Baronet Downhill
(1843–1919)

Admiral James Andrew Thomas

Hervey Ronald
5th Baronet Downhill
(1872–1924)

Sir Hervey John Bruce
6th Baronet Downhill
(1919–1971)

Sir Hervey James Hugh Bruce
7th Baronet Downhill

Percy Robert = Aletheia Paget
(1872–1924)

Gervase

William

John, Lord Hervey
(1696–1743)

The BRUCE Family Tree

The 3rd Baronet's arms

Henry William

Stewart Crawford

Robert

Lloyd Stewart = Janie Skene
(1829–1886)

Captain Wilfrid
(1874–1953)

Rev. Rosslyn = Rachel Gurney
(1871–1956)

Kathleen = Captain Scott
(of Antarctic)

Henry James = Tamara Karsavina
'Benjie'
(1880–1951)

Erroll

Merlin

Peter Scott

Nikita

The Reverend Sir Henry Hervey Bruce

(First Baronet Downhill)

HENRY HERVEY BRUCE was a cousin to the Earl-Bishop (see family tree on page 102). He was also the brother of Frideswide, to whom, as Mrs Mussenden, the Bishop dedicated the Temple. So it is hardly surprising that the Bishop was well-disposed towards him when as a young man he entertained hopes of marriage to Letitia Barnard, the grand-daughter of one of Derry's previous bishops. The Barnards had not been greatly impressed by the prospects of young Bruce as a son-in-law. Having just come down from Trinity College with the intention of entering the church, he did not offer much by way of financial security for his would-be bride; but then in 1786 the Bishop, with his characteristic generosity where impoverished curates were concerned, settled on him a yearly income of £400, and the incumbency of Tamlaghfinlagan, Ballykelly. In a letter shortly after, from Venice, he wrote:

> 'My dearest Harry, you have done perfectly right, in not quitting yr dearest Letitia while her spirits needed yr presence & yr own spirit could support hers. She was yr first parish. Ballykelly is at best but a lawful concubine & very secondary to your true legitimate & carnal wife for you were a man before you became a Parson & therefore conjugal duties are prior to clerical ones.'

Henry Hervey Bruce became the Bishop's steward at Downhill, and managed both the estate and the diocese during that great traveller's long absences on the Continent. They corresponded copiously on all the details of running the Bishop's affairs, and the Bishop usually addressed his letters to 'Dearest Harry'. A huge body of this writing concerned the renewal of leases and the collection of rents – which comprised much of the Bishop's Irish income – but frequently, and especially towards the end of his life, there are also remarks on the

Derry cathedral,with its contentious spire.

other resident clergy. Robert McGhee, the 'thorough-paced sinner' of the Downhill book-keeping (see page 42) and who was the rector at Dromore, comes in for heavy censure: 'Remove McGhee out of the diocese as soon as possible – 'tis a rotten sheep may infect others.' Soden, who had been Archdeacon for a period, fares no better: 'One may trust Soden with anything but one's purse and one's bottle.' Bruce's correspondence may have been full of tedious business but it had other interest too. One of the preoccupations of these later letters was the possible collapse of the Bishop's fine spire on Derry Cathedral, caused – according to him – by the deliberate neglect of the Dean.

> '. . . the only danger to the steeple must appear from the fissures or gaps being wider. That to remedy this an Iron Cramp passed from One wall to the other is a most certain security against the two walls swerving . . . many years ago Mr Shanahan apprized the Dean and Mayor of the necessity to glaze the openings in the steeple which has ever been most intentionally neglected from the hatred the Dean bears me.'

Harry evidently had a great deal more than his normal pastoral duties to fulfil.

Bruce was the rector at Tamlaghfinlagan during all this time, although he was informed in 1791 that he was to inherit Downhill; this was in a letter that the Bishop had written to him from Annan in Scotland where, smitten with gout on his way to the Continent, he had felt sufficiently unwell to write his will. It seems very odd that the Bishop should leave all his Irish property away from his immediate family, but at the same time in keeping with the character of the man – he had fallen out with his wife and eldest son, and also he may have felt that it was a way of honouring Bruce's sister who, as Mrs Mussenden, had died so very young. The Bishop was to stick to his decision, even though he was to live on in his usual vigorous way for another 12 years, and he confirmed matters by adding a codicil to this will in 1794; writing from Aosta in Italy he also left to Bruce all his works of art collected in Europe, and all his estates in England which were not entailed. Most of the collection of art not then in Ireland was destined not to fall to the fortunate Harry Bruce, as it was seized by the French in Rome in 1798 and to this day no one knows of its fate. This is partly because no one knows exactly what it comprised, no catalogue having survived; the Bishop valued the collection at £18,000, and even allowing for a little exaggeration on his part, this represents a huge sum in the late eighteenth century.

Harry Bruce came into the Bishop's property in 1803 when the latter died. He seems to have preferred to live in Downhill, rather than at Ballyscullion, which was to be partly dismantled in 1813 in order to evade the payment of window tax. Sampson's Survey mentions his keeping up the estate and putting it to good use: 'The view from the Strand Lodge [The Lion Gate] displays at once the beauty of the Grounds in front of the House, the rich verdure of the grass giving pasture to fine large Ayrshire cows and Merino sheep.' The property also embraced the parishes of Dunboe, Grangebeg, Ardbra, Kileranahan, Ballyscullion, Banagher, Donakiddy, Drinah and Magilligan. Harry Bruce built the Glebe House for Aghadowey and was certainly resident there in 1791. The house was called Blackheath, and was probably designed by Shanahan. Bruce continued his duty at Ballykelly however, driving there every Sunday with some magnificence in a coach accompanied by four postillions.

Bruce was created a baronet in 1804, a rare honour for an Irish clergyman. He had three sons and six daughters. One son, James Robertson, succeeded to the title and the property on his father's death, thus becoming the second baronet. Letitia, Lady Bruce, died in 1816 and was buried in the family vault which her husband had built in Dunboe churchyard in 1810. The Rev. Sir Henry Hervey Bruce followed in 1822.

The Bruce family mausoleum in Old Dunboe churchyard.

Sir Henry Hervey Bruce

(Third Baronet Downhill)

SIR HENRY HERVEY BRUCE inherited Downhill and the title in 1836. He had been an officer in the Life Guards, and is supposed to have been requested to resign after attending a wedding without leave, a breach of discipline which, if true, he made up for later in his running of the Downhill household and in his attitude to his sons and grandchildren. We receive a vivid picture of this stalwart Tory gentleman from the recollections of his grandson Henry James Bruce ('Benjie' in the family) who lived at Downhill as a child and spent many holidays there in later life.

Sir Hervey took a deep interest in the estate and in the area as a whole. He stood for parliament on several occasions and was returned for Coleraine twice: 1862–74 and again in 1880–85. His politics were severely loyalist and admitted of only one party. 'There *is* only the Conservative party. The rest are rebels.' To reinforce this he had apparently been known, during sessions of parliament, to climb on the benches and crow like a cockerel if a Liberal member was attempting to speak. (And we complain today of parliamentary debates sounding like a farmyard!) According to his grandson, a picture of Gladstone, the Liberal Prime Minister, was hung at Downhill in that room where 'photographs are inappropriate'. His electioneering activities brought him into head-on conflict with Samuel McCurdy Greer, Minister of Dunboe Presbyterian Church, staunch Liberal and very much the champion of tenants' rights, who was to beat him in the contest for one of County Londonderry's two seats in 1857. Other public commitments included serving as magistrate, and as Lord-Lieutenant of Londonderry, and as being the chairman of Londonderry's first County Council. On the estate he had built the Keeper's Lodge in the 1850s, the 'Twelve Apostles' in 1882 – estate workers' cottages at the Castlerock end of the demesne – and the Downhill National School in 1872. In 1871 he bought out the Clothworkers' property in the area and thus became the largest single landowner; the estate then including Castlerock itself, in the development of which Sir Hervey took a particular interest, requiring, for example, all new building there to be of a certain quality and size. He was strongly instrumental in the building and endowment of the Castlerock parish church, Christ Church.

It was in the third baronet's time that Downhill Castle itself was severely damaged by a fire. It broke out on 16 May 1851 and devastated the building and a great deal of the Bishop's priceless and irreplacable treasures within. A local inhabitant produced a set of verses on the occasion which, whatever they lack in poetic craftsmanship, do at least give an idea of the scale of the blaze:

'The men all wrought courageous,
But proved of no avail;
The flames extended rapidly,
Forced by a northern gale.
For eight and forty hours
The[y] beat all human skill,
Before the flames abated
In the Castle of Downhill.'

How the fire started has never been established, although Sir Hervey suspected arson (see page 19), but the great house was never to be the same again, changing almost at a stroke from the splendidly appointed episcopal palace to late Victorian country house and shooting lodge (see page 20).

Sir Hervey was married in 1842 – significantly, on 12 July – to Marianne Clifton, the only daughter of a wealthy Nottinghamshire family; the popular idea was that her dowry was equal in value to her own weight (wearing her wedding dress) in gold. Whatever the truth of that, it was a fact that the Bruces eventually inherited the Clifton estates, and the fine mansion there, dating originally from the 1600s, which became the family's second home – 'Downhill for the grouse, Clifton for the partridges, both for pheasants', as recorded by Benjie. Lady Margaret, like her husband, also took a keen interest in the estate, especially in the education of the tenants' children. Lady Bruce was also vaguely rumoured to have had love-affairs, though her grandson seems to have thought it rather unlikely. There is a piece of local folk lore which concerns a foreign butler who had mysteriously disappeared from the Castle – murdered in the more lurid versions – possibly because of too close a relationship with the mistress of the house (see Folk legend and the supernatural, page 179).

The Castle at the turn of the century, a view showing Lady Erne's seat in the foreground and the last vestiges of the extensive planting in the grounds. On the right hay is apparently being saved.

Decidedly, the rumour was a drawback to the baronet's electioneering campaigns.

In its heyday, life in the Castle had a certain magnificence. Benjie's recollections paint a picture of contrasting values: if, on the one hand, the young Bruces had the run of the grounds and the glen and the strand, life within doors was very much more restricted. Everyone dressed for dinner, whether there were guests or not, and Sundays must have been particularly severe, from the walk to church at Castlerock through the weary day to the evening prayers in the dining room, with the whole staff in attendance, and the head of the household reading interminable passages from the New Testament inextricably mixed up with Bentley's commentaries. The heavy Victorian atmosphere prevailing in the house may have attained a certain sombre grandeur at times, but we may be sure that it had little of the light-hearted elegance that may have filled the place in its founder's lifetime; the Bishop's fine Irish silver was still used at meal times, and Sir Hervey is recorded as having a good appreciation of fine wines. He had a cordial dislike of both tobacco and animals, and was apparently given to writing a kind of school report in the form of a letter after a visit from his son and family: the children were admonished for walking up and down the passages like Dragoons, or for 'slunging about with hands in bottom of pockets' while their father was indicted for 'coming to meals with hands fresh from playing with cat or dog'. Once, having invited his young nephew Rosslyn to stay during the summer holidays, he sent on after him the rather small bill he had incurred for the hire of a bicycle. He had firm ideas about the conduct of the clergy: to the same nephew, about to take holy orders, he wrote 'I did not look to see how long your sermon lasted when you were here. I should say about twenty minutes. Your father's time used to be twelve. You can put a good deal in twelve minutes if you go the right way. . .' He thought that holding up the collection plate 'looked silly' and usually put into it a sovereign for a ten minute sermon, but only half a sovereign for twenty! Significently, his favourite reading was (like that of Jane Austen's Sir Walter Elliot) Debrett's Peerage.

Lady Bruce died in 1891 and was buried in the Bruce mausoleum in old Dunboe churchyard. Sir Hervey was deeply affected by her loss and apparently used to visit the churchyard on a daily basis; to make it easier to do this he had a small door cut in the demesne wall between the Bishop's and Lion Gates. Both door and wall were demolished when the main road was altered in 1963. Kathleen Bruce (Rosslyn's sister) visited Downhill about this time and recalled being taken by Sir Hervey to see the grave, and his saying to her 'My dear, would you like to live here? You could pour out the tea and mend the china and things . . . You wouldn't be in my way.' Sir Hervey died in 1907 aged 87 and was buried in Dunboe churchyard; on the headstone of the grave are the words of the hymn:

> 'Weary of earth and laden with my sin,
> I look at Heaven and long to enter in'

Hervey Juckes Lloyd Bruce

(Fourth Baronet Downhill)

THE FOURTH BARONET was one of the more colourful characters in an already colourful family. Like many of that family he was educated at Eton and served in the army, reaching the rank of Lieutenant Colonel in the Coldstream Guards. He was married in 1872 to Ellen Maud Ricardo – known in the family as 'Nellie' – and had four sons, the first two twins. He inherited the title in 1907 and thus came into the property of Downhill, where one might assume the late summer Bruce holiday (July to September), was then spent in somewhat less severe style than in the time of his father, the third baronet. Our best picture of him comes from the pen of his youngest son, Henry James Bruce ('Benjie'), in whose autobiography *Silken Dalliance* anecdotes of his father abound. For one thing, his appearance was rather remarkable: his English father-in-law is reported as maintaining that 'Hervey wears clothes you wouldn't take off a scarecrow, puts a Malmaison carnation in his buttonhole and thinks he's well dressed.' The buttonholes were very important: 'the nearer in size to a prima donna's last night's bouquet the better'. His manner of dressing when in the country, combined with his great love of animals, on one occasion led to his being mistaken for a tramp by the maid at one of his tenant's houses; under the curious outfit he was carrying a pet monkey. If he was less of a public figure than the third baronet, it is pleasant to know that he was at least given to visiting his tenants, and on foot. Among the other pets, his son remembered parrots, a hare that walked with the retrievers, a blackbird which lived on friendly terms with the cat, and a tame grouse. Perhaps Benjie's best story illustrates the fourth baronet's attitudes to human beings as opposed to his friends the animals; being seated next to a dowager at a meal he is recorded as having said 'May I peel this peach for you? It's too ripe for the monkey.'

His son describes him as a man of gruff exterior and biting comment, but on at least one occasion recalls a tender moment, when on leaving Downhill for the last time in 1914 on the eve of the First

The fourth baronet, reproduced from his son's autobiography *Silken Dalliance.*

World War, seeing his father moved to tears. Thunder clouds had been gathering over Ireland at this time too, with Ulster's resistance to the Home Rule bill. British naval ships had been sent to Belfast Lough in a show of strength and at one time during that year a destroyer had been stationed in Lough Foyle, among other reasons to keep an eye on Downhill, possibly on the suspicion that the Castle might be used to store smuggled weapons intended for use by the Ulster Volunteer Force. Whether the fourth baronet's support for the movement was very much more than tacit, one can easily imagine that having his home swept with a searchlight from the sea was not likely to make him change his opinions. Certainly he is recorded as having inspected the local Coleraine division of the UVF on a visit to the Castle, and his eldest son, Sir Ronald – later to become the fifth baronet – was a captain in the force.

Lady Ellen Bruce's personality must have been the equal of her husband; she appears in photographs with the Articlave Boy's Brigade when their colours were presented at the Castle, and also inspecting UVF nurses in 1914. She was chief of the North Derry Women's Ambulance Force, and was awarded the OBE for her work during the First War. There were more domestic attributes too; her son Benjie describes her as being a phenomenal knitter, using 'six needles and goodness knows how many different balls of wool.' This description is set in part of the servants' quarters of the Castle in the time of the third baronet, a room known in the family as 'the Robbers' Cave', and was the only place he permitted his sons to smoke. Lady Ellen was also interested in photography and apparently had a dark room installed in the house. Her son is slightly disparaging about her painting, remarking that she produced 'an occasional well-meant water-colour' – one such was a very charming picture of Christ Church in Castlerock, where the Bruces wor-

The south front of the Castle, with members of the Articlave Boys Brigade in the foreground, photographed in 1911.

Christ Church, Castlerock, from the watercolour by Lady Ellen Bruce, painted before the clock was installed in the spire.

shipped at that time. (See also her painting of the Castle facing the first chapter of this book.)

After the First World War, during which the Bruces were absent from Downhill, Sir Hervey visited Benjie in his last diplomatic post in Tangiers. Lady Bruce had thought that the warm climate – very much a change from that at Downhill – would be good for the chest trouble from which he was suffering. However it was not to be so, and the fourth baronet died there in 1919, and the title passed to the 'eldest' of the twins, Sir Ronald.

Henry James Bruce

('Benjie')

HENRY JAMES BRUCE was the fourth son of the fourth baronet. Born in the Bruce's London house, 6 St James's Square in 1880, he spent much of his childhood at Downhill, returning there frequently for holidays during adult life. His time at Downhill as a boy he described vividly in the first part of his autobiography *Silken Dalliance.* Just before the turn of the century, the place was ideal for young 'Benjie', as he was called in the family, and his elder brothers: Magilligan strand he described as 'a bather's dream and a child's paradise'. In those days the young Bruces could regard it as their own 'private beach with never a soul in sight'. Then there was the fishing, the shooting – pheasant and grouse in those days – and 'unlimited scope in the glens for the woodmanship we boys were expert in, especially the bonfire part.'

As for schooling, young Benjie was sent to Eton where, by his own account, he certainly learnt a great deal about rowing, if nothing else. The school holidays were divided between Downhill and Clifton, the family's Nottinghamshire home. Leaving Eton at the comparatively late age of nineteen (his services had been required in the rowing eight) and having fixed on diplomacy for a career, he spent the following years learning the various languages necessary for the diplomatic examination, both by living in France, Germany and Italy, and through cramming in London. The London part of his studies instilled him with a great love of the theatre, which perhaps indirectly was later to lead him to his choice of wife. He joined the Foreign Office in 1904 and after serving as a junior for nearly two years began his diplomatic career proper as an attaché in Vienna.

The Vienna of this period was an all but legendary city, the political and cultural centre of a huge but declining empire. Bruce's work in the Embassy was not, by his own admission, highly pressured, but gradually his responsibilities grew until he became the Ambassador's private secretary. Among other duties this took him to Marienbad on two occasions to be in attendance on King Edward VII. His respect and admiration for the king were assured from their first meeting: 'I knew your grandfather quite well' were the first royal

Bruce children on Magilligan strand; the two elder boys are possibly the twins, Ronald and Percy.

words, to which the recipient added parenthetically 'I expect he knew a suaver side of him than I did'. The king certainly appreciated his work and awarded him the Victorian Order as well as presenting him with a silver cigarette case. His next post was in Berlin, which he found dull and constrained after the social gaiety of Vienna. He was appointed Commercial Secretary, the first of that breed in Berlin, and found that there were some attractions to be found in 'this infernal city': the theatrical productions of Max Reinhardt, the first flight of one of the earliest airships and more meetings with the famous, including the Kaiser, the Crown Prince and – of more real interest to him – Conan Doyle and Puccini, 'a delightfully simple, childlike and light-hearted person'. This existence continued until 1913 when the ambassador reluctantly released him for a new post in St Petersburg, allowing only time for 'a fortnight's fresh air', which as he said, 'I was sure of getting that at Downhill'.

It was in St Petersburg that he met and married Tamara Karsavina, a ballerina who danced in the Diaghalev company. Apart from a brief meeting in London, when she was appearing at Covent Garden and he was on his way back to Downhill for a short holiday, their

courting took place in St Petersburg. With the First World War tearing Europe and the old order apart it must have been an uncertain time for a young couple, and when matters came to a head with the Russian Revolution they were lucky to escape with their lives. The final flight in July 1918 was a close-run thing. Hampered, or perhaps helped, by the presence of a two-year-old son Nikita, they managed to get to Murmansk through a mixture of luck, courage and the fame of Tamara Karsavina. At the port they found a British merchant ship and, apart from the U-boat threat in the North Sea, the rest was

(Left) H.J.Bruce, 'Benjie' and his wife Tamara (above) who was a prima ballerina in the Ballet Russe.

relatively plain sailing. Despite the war, the revolution and this last hair-raising experience, Bruce seems to have loved St Petersburg and been genuinely fond of the 'ordinary' Russian people, whom he found 'temperamentally rather akin to the Irish.' He relates having once 'seen a *droshky* driving down the Millionaya, the Park Lane of St Petersburg, its only occupant a pig'.

Then came a year in Tangiers, after which he left the diplomatic service in order to follow Tamara's career in the ballet, to which she had been lured back again by Diaghalev. While his wife was fully engaged in being a star, Benjie took a bank clerk's job at £4 a week, illustrating a certain degree of humility in one who had previously been a First Secretary in a British Embassy. However diplomacy of a sort was to call again, and he found himself in Sofia, Bulgaria, as the

Secretary General of an Interallied Commission. In between tours on the Continent and to America, Tamara and young Nik joined him in Bulgaria, until 1926 when the job finished and the family returned to London, just in time for the General Strike. This was to provide Benjie with his next job, which only lasted for nine days; he was put in charge of the signal box at Fenchurch Street station and despite its being 'the size of a cricket pitch' and having about 150 levers, he only made one mistake during his spell of duty. After a jobless interim of five years, while Tamara danced and then set up a school for ballet, and while he reconsidered his career and whether banking should be his new *métier*, an important job in banking suddenly came his way. He was appointed by the Bank of England to be adviser to the National Bank of Hungary. This was a job of enormous responsibility and he seems to have absorbed the necessary knowledge of economics while travelling to post by train and then while actually doing the job itself. Despite nervous beginnings in 1931 he grew to enjoy the work which, in its most terrifying aspect, included reporting to the finance committee of the League of Nations; on the first occasion he wrote to Tamara 'I'm sure I should have been much less worried on the eve of my execution'. Tamara joined him later in Budapest, where they set up house and by his own account were very contented until returning to Britain just before the Second World War burst over Europe. They survived the war years in London, and Nikita, who had interrupted the start of a career in the theatre to join the army, survived the evacuation of Dunkirk. Benjie wrote two books of autobiography, the first *Silken Dalliance* was published in 1946, the second *Thirty Dozen Moons* in 1949, both sadly now out of print. Sadly, because quite apart from the cherished memories of Downhill, they are charmingly written books on their own account, full of erudition lightly carried, of anecdote relating to the famous, of humour and of the diplomat's insight into historical events. As a sample of his style, here is how he summed up his feelings after the Munich Crisis: 'Unless, in these days, you have mighty strength, sweet reason will likely land you in disaster. This has been true since Adam walked out of Eden. It will remain true until the Garden is reopened to the public.' He died in 1951, after the Downhill Estates had finally passed out of the Bruce family's hands, and the Castle itself had had its roof removed, the start of a slow but inexorable dissolution.

Some other members of the Bruce family

James Robertson Bruce 1788–1836
became the second baronet in 1822. He is the only baronet not to have had the name Hervey. His elder brother, who had been christened Hervey, died in 1787 before his father 'Harry' Bruce, and so the title went to Sir James. He married in 1819, to Ellen Hesketh, a lady from Denbighshire. Sir James continued with the great scheme of tree-planting which his father had carried on from its initiation by the Bishop; over 50,000 trees being added to the existing numbers. Lewis's Topographical Dictionary of Ireland for the period states that 'In the glens, the plantations are extensive, beautifully laid out, and ornamented with rustic buildings and bridges.' Sir James also established a school for the children of his tenants, which was built within the demesne behind the Bishop's Gate. In the 1830s there was an outbreak of cholera in the countryside, which concerned Sir James sufficiently to suspend the privilege to Roman Catholics of being permitted to worship in the Mussenden Temple crypt. He subscribed money to the medical dispensary in Coleraine, a very much needed amenity in the days before the NHS. Of his four sons, perhaps the most remarkable was the eldest, Henry Hervey, who succeeded to the title and was to be master of Downhill for longer that any, either before or since.

Hervey Ronald Bruce 1872–1924
'Ronnie' was the 'elder' of the fourth baronet's twin sons. When he became the fifth baronet in 1919, he inherited the property at Downhill, while the younger twin, Percy, came into that of Clifton, the other Bruce home in Nottinghamshire. As a boy, his summer holidays would have been spent at Downhill as described by the younger brother Benjie (see page 154), occasionally being enlivened by visitors such as his cousin Rosslyn who came in 1894 to share in such modern pastimes as bicycle excursions. Ronald went into the army, serving both in the Irish Guards and the 14th Irish Rifles, reaching

Sir Ronald Bruce, the fifth baronet, in the uniform of the Irish guards.

the rank of major. He fought in the Boer War, and was in command of the North Londonderry Regiment of the UVF prior to 1914. He was married twice, in 1903 to Ruth Okeover (cousin Rosslyn officiating) then in 1916 to Margaret Jackson. In 1924 he took his family away from Downhill because of the uncertain political climate and settled temporarily in Eastbourne. It was in Eastbourne that he died as the result of a strange accident, suffering a fall from the marine parade during a particularly spectacular thunderstorm. He was buried at Herstmonceux, Rosslyn's church.

James Andrew Thomas Bruce 1846–1921
was the fourth baronet's brother. His career, like that of several other Bruces, was in the Royal Navy, in which he achieved the rank of Admiral. (A great-uncle, Henry William Bruce, had also reached the same rank. His memorial plaque can be seen in Belaghy Church.) Although his visits to Downhill were rare, his nephew, Benjie, wrote affectionately of him as being very much the master of

the ships he commanded, but not so much the master of the domestic sphere, where the real ruler was his wife, Aunt Philippa. Part of the affection was due to the way in which 'little uncle Admiral Sir Jimmie Bruce', as Rosslyn once referred to him, had accepted Benjie's marriage to Tamara Karsavina of the Ballet Russe: after the initial misgivings – anything to do with the stage being then regarded, at the least, as of dubious morality – the Russian 'ballet-girl' soon became a favourite with him, 'the little fellah' as he was to call her.

He was buried at Clifton churchyard in Nottinghamshire.

Rosslyn Bruce 1871–1956

whose connection with Downhill was slightly less that his cousins, deserves more than just a passing mention, if only because of his remarkable character and life, which was very much that of a Bruce. His father was the third baronet's brother, Lloyd. Following his marriage in 1863 to Janie Skene, the honeymoon was spent at Downhill; Rosslyn's mother wrote 'Lady Bruce and I get on famously', adding however that 'they all sit up so late at night'. Rosslyn was born at Barton-in-Fabis, not very far from the Bruce's Clifton home, and was educated in England. When his father died in 1886, uncle Hervey, attending the funeral, noticed that Rosslyn had a ferret in his pocket, and apparently decided that he would be a good companion for his grandsons at Downhill during the summer holidays. This seems a little strange, given the third baronet's well-known distaste for animals; how much greater his disapproval would have been had he discovered that his young nephew, on a later holiday visit, had become a convinced 'Home-ruler'! He went to Oxford to study for the church and became an enthusiastic speaker in the Union, where his light-heartedness and humour enlivened even very serious debates, and he was only just beaten to the presidency by Hilaire Belloc. He served as a curate first of all in north Derbyshire, and then at St Anne's in London's Soho, very much a baptism of fire for a budding clergyman, Soho being as tough an area in the 1890s as it is today. He was a popular preacher, and his popularity may be judged from the fact that his last sermon in St Anne's was preached to a congregation of over 1,500 (the church's normal capacity was 900). Rosslyn had been ordained in 1898, but his first parish was at Clifton, the living of which was, of course, in the gift of uncle Hervey. In 1908 he married Rachel Gurney; only a few weeks after his sister,

The Rev. Rosslyn Bruce and *Aerial*; he hunted regularly with the Rufford.

Kathleen, had been married to Captain Scott (Scott of the Antarctic). Although idyllic, Clifton did not provide this most energetic Christian ultimately with sufficient of a challenge, so the next parish was Edgbaston, and was then followed in 1923 by Herstmonceux in Sussex.

One of Rosslyn's lifelong and most endearing qualities was his total devotion to animals. He was an acknowledged authority on breeding Skye Terriers – he sold one to Queen Victoria – and smooth fox terriers – one went to King George V. During his college days he had even kept an elephant, among other creatures. At Clifton there was enough livestock to open a private zoo, and at one stage in his career he had bred green mice. This latter achievement was not part of any of his numerous practical jokes, but was a piece of serious study on line breeding for which, incidentally, he was made a Fellow of the Linnaean Society. The kind of clergyman who rides to hounds or, in the course of his address ('sermon' was a word he disliked) released a dove into his church to illustrate the flight of love, is something of a rarity today.

Kathleen Bruce

Rosslyn's sister was a gifted artist and sculptor, who had studied in Paris in Rodin's atelier. Kathleen's marriage to Captain Scott was tragically cut short after only four years when he perished in the heroic South Pole expedition of 1912. Their son was Peter Scott, whose distinguished career as a naturalist and whose artistic abilities must owe much to the Bruce side of the family.

In all their history the Bruces have never been very far from the sea: CAPTAIN WILFRED BRUCE, brother of Kathleen and of Rosslyn, was the navigator on the *Terra Nova*, the ship which took Captain Scott on his last Antarctic expedition. He had a distinguished naval career in the Second World War, particularly with the minesweeping arm of the service out of Lowestoft. MERLIN BRUCE, Rosslyn's eldest son, was a Commander in the Fleet Air Arm during the Second World War, and also served on aircraft carriers during the Korean War. In his early days at sea, he wore a coat that belonged to Captain Scott. ERROLL BRUCE, Rosslyn's second son, also had a naval career, serving on submarines in the Second World War. In peace time he was a keen ocean racer and in 1950 skippered *Samuel Pepys*, the winning yacht in the Bermuda to Plymouth transatlantic race. Then there was GERVASE BRUCE who was nephew to the fifth baronet and who, as a young midshipman of only 15 died in action in 1914 on HMS *Monmouth* at the battle of Coronel. (For those interested in the long arm of coincidence, it is interesting to note that the Bishop's remains were brought back to Britain on board HMS *Monmouth*, and that a ship of the same name was under the command of his brother Augustus for some time.)

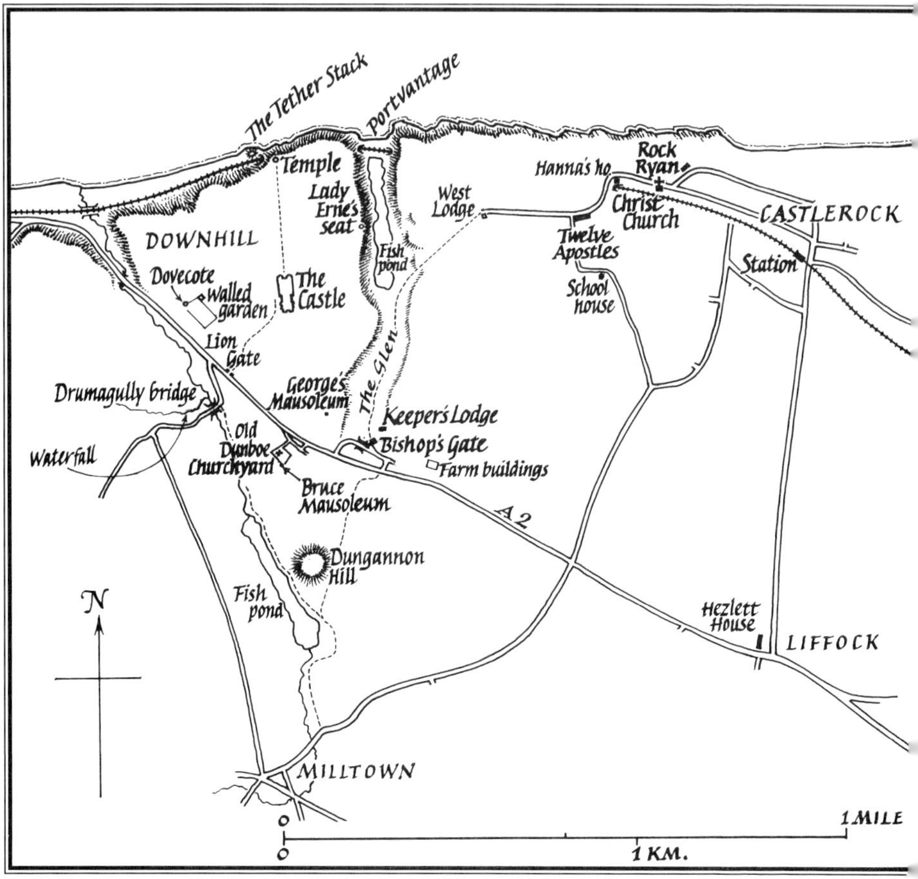

Map of the Downhill and Castlerock area.

Bruce family building ventures

IF MUCH of the Bishop's inspiration to build sprang from a need for self-aggrandisement and an eye to posterity, and rather less from a sense of *pro bono publico*, the same might be said of some of his heirs – though on a much diminished scale. The Bruce family were considerable builders, but lacking the Bishop's enormous income, their efforts were more confined to consolidation and to improving his legacy.

The Rev. 'Harry' Bruce, who inherited Downhill from the Bishop in 1803, had for many years previously been the steward of the estates as well as acting as the Bishop's agent in matters secular within the see of Derry. He was moreover the vicar at Finlagan, Ballykelly, and continued his duties to his flock there after inheriting the Castle. As rector at Finlagan he made great improvements to the glebe house there, but this was as nothing to the glebe house for the parish of Aghadowey, 'Blackheath'. It is thought that Shanahan was the architect he employed for this house, although there is no evidence in writing to support this, only the characteristic style of the building and its general high quality of workmanship – as indeed it should have been, having cost £1,756 upon completion in 1794.

Apart from continuing with any of the demesne buildings at Downhill, Harry Bruce was responsible for the finishing off of the northern curtain walls of the Castle, for although these were started in the Bishop's lifetime, they were not completed, with their curious false perspective and military-looking crenellations, until after.

With Sir James Robertson Bruce, the second baronet, it is difficult to ascribe any building work other than his help with the building of a school for boys and girls on Downhill Estate land. The school was established in 1824 (costing £119 to build) by the Kildare Society, an organisation devoted to the education of the Irish poor and originally supported by all denominations. In addition to giving the land Sir James also subsidised the teachers' salaries. Though the second baronet did not leave any very grand buildings, he certainly believed in the proper maintenance of the existing ones, and gave sums of money for the improvement both of the established

(Left) the sundial dated 1823 on St Paul's church, Articlave. (Right) 'chalet' style bargeboards on the gable of Rock Ryan. (Right below) the Twelve Apostles, Castlerock.

Church's and Presbyterian's buildings. He opened the Glen once a year to the public, and permitted the taking of any fallen timber.

The next of the Bruces to inherit Downhill was rather different: the vigorous Sir Henry Hervey, third Baronet Downhill, built largely and indulged in politics largely, often finding himself in conflict, both direct and indirect, with the Clothworkers' Company and the Liberal Presbyterian Minister Samuel McCurdy Greer. (This period and its political ramifications has been admirably covered by Alison McCaughan in *Heath, Hearth and Heart.*) The development of Castlerock in the mid-nineteenth century from a small village to a prosperous resort town was due as much to the impetus given by the Bruces as to the arrival of the railway. The most prominent landmark of the town in 1870 was the newly built church of Christ Church, in its size and confidence demonstrating the expansion of the town; St Paul's in Articlave having become too small to serve the growing C. of I. congregation. Castlerock had been part of Dunboe parish but as it had grown so much it was formed into a district parish with its own vicar (the Reverend James Armstrong) in 1868. Until Christ Church was finished, worship was conducted in the house known as Rock Ryan, which was originally a bathing lodge. The Bruces endowed the church and there are many memorials and windows to members of the family; a peal of bells was given to the church in 1891 in memory of Lady Bruce, wife of the third baronet. The architect of Christ Church was F. W. Porter, who was based in

London and did much work for the Clothworkers' Company. It is said locally that one of the workers on Christ Church was one Joe Brady, later to be executed in connection with the 'Invincibles' of the Phœnix Park Murders of 1882.

But Castlerock was graced by other Bruce-built or Bruce-inspired edifices. One of the more remarkable of these is the line of houses known as the 'Twelve Apostles'. They were built in 1882 to house the families of the estate workers. The 'Tudor Cottage' design, which

The Keeper's Lodge and (below) Downhill school

looks as though it has been taken from an English model village, was by F. H. Godwin. Close by stands the Downhill school, also built by the Bruces and finished in 1872, a date proudly cut in a roundel on one of the gables. The gate lodge at the Castlerock edge of the estate was probably erected in this period, as was the little house to the east of the Twelve Apostles known as 'Hanna's House'. The Hanna in question had been a housemaid at the Castle, and lived to be 95.

As the Bruces owned so much land and wielded so much power in the locality at the time, they were also able to influence how Castlerock grew up. Several of the taller houses in the main street show the

Bruce style, dark basalt with pale freestone trim about windows and doors, and at least three stories high – the family was said to have not permitted the building of anything of a less imposing height.

Going further back to the 1850s there is a handsome little house behind the Bishop's Gate Lodge which was built for the third baronet's gamekeeper; properly known as the Keeper's Lodge it is now more usually called the 'Kennels'. To the east of this house are the estate farmyards with their attached buildings for animals, the storage of fodder and wagons, all probably erected about 1840.

Trees and shrubs

IT WAS CHARACTERISTIC of the Bishop that he should commence the building of Downhill Castle before giving a thought to the landscaping. Indeed, it almost seems as though the process was initiated by Michael Shanahan, the Bishop's architect. In 1776 when Arthur Young passed by, he found the house well advanced, but 'it stands on a bold shore where a tree is a rarity', and it was not until 1778 that Shanahan was writing to his employer about tree planting and gardening matters:

> 'On receipt of your lordships favour of the 5th June I wrote to Mr. King at Lord Enniskillen to procure in time an Ample Store of Tamarisk, laburnams, Myrtles, roses of every kind, Sweet briar, etc etc as your Lordship order'd, this is the only Scheme I approve of, that has as yet been propos'd for adorning the Downhill, the walks around the demesne being planted with Shrubs of this kind, will look very delightfull and soon come to perfection without any danger of suffering by Storms.'

The exposed position was of course one of the main problems, as Shanahan was at pains to point out: 'I am certain had your Lordship known the Site you would not say, you would stop it until your return, as no plantation can be made round it, nor any planting within until the walls are first built.'

It was a huge undertaking; Shanahan remarks in the same letter that 'it is but a folly to think your lordship could live here without a garden . . . The gardiner has 20 men at work every day, he attends them close, and I think he does your Lordship justice.' While the 'gardiner' supervised his small army, Shanahan himself was engaged in a little agriculture, providing fodder for his horses: 'as for straw and oats, the quantity I sowed in the obelisk [Mausoleum] field I hope will be sufft. for my purpose – '. By the spring of 1783 when the Bishop returned to Ireland things were evidently still continuing at a great pace. Arthur Young, the Bishop's neighbour at his English seat at Ickworth, Suffolk, no doubt offered him plenty of advice on horticultural matters, and in return received enthusiastic reports from Downhill:

> 'Whenever you are vapid, if ever those *petillants* spirits of yours are so, come and imbibe some fixed, or rather unfixed, air at the Downhill, where a tree is no longer a rarity, since above 200,000 have this winter been planted in the glens around my house. Come and enjoy the rapidity & the success wth which I have converted sixty acres of moor by the medium of 200 spades into a green carpet sprinkled with white clover; am I not an adept in national dialect? Come and enjoy some mountains converted into arable. . .'

The Bishop had evidently learned, as 'a willing disciple' of his friend Young, of the value of lime as a fertiliser, and he continues in the same letter, 'The limestone is at the bottom of the hill, the turf at the top; what gold may this chemistry produce?' By 1785 the Bishop was writing about an even larger quantity of trees to his daughter Mary: 'Downhill is becoming Elegance itself – 300,000 trees without Doors upon all the banks & upon all the rocks. . .'

There was a probably unconscious irony here, in that many of the trees the Bishop is so proud of came from Lord Erne – Lady Mary's husband – at the time of the letter they were already estranged. Given the very large number of trees planted it seems a little implausible that they should all have come from the same source. It may not be too fanciful to suppose that the Bishop might also have applied to the family of another of his sons-in-law for plants – John Thomas Foster, Elizabeth's husband, whose cousin's collection of plants at Oriel Temple in Co. Louth was one of the largest in the country. (He was also primarily instrumental in the founding of the Glasnevin Botanical Gardens.) Certainly by the year 1790, he was able to offer for sale some 250 varieties of trees and shrubs.

The extent of the planting can be gauged from the account given by Sampson for the Statistical Survey of Co. Londonderry in 1802; among others he listed the following – ash, mountain ash, oak, five varieties of willow, horse chestnut, lime, spruce, larch, pine, yew, wych elm, alder, whortleberry, broom, tamarisk, laburnum, myrtle, and sweetbriar. Sycamore was conspicuous by its absence. Whitethorn had also been planted generally ('Quicks' in Shanahan's memos) to provide hedging and much needed wind-breaks. Under the Bishop's successor, Harry Bruce, 39,000 more trees were put in and a further 52,000 by his son James Robertson Bruce.

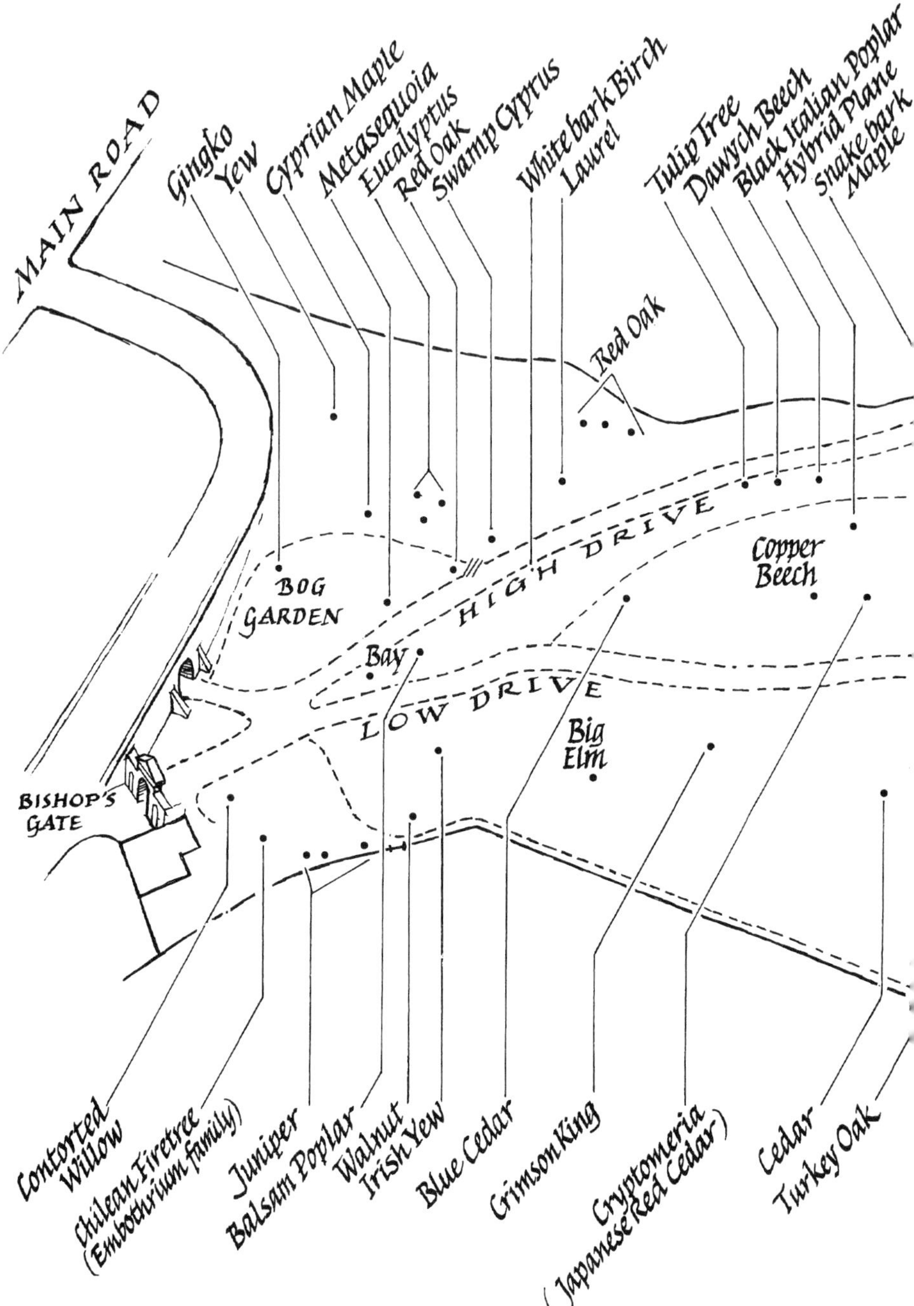

MAIN ROAD
Gingko
Yew
Cyprian Maple
Metasequoia
Eucalyptus
Red Oak
Swamp Cyprus
White bark Birch
Laurel
Tulip Tree
Dawych Beech
Black Italian Poplar
Hybrid Plane
Snake bark Maple
Red Oak
HIGH DRIVE
Copper Beech
BOG GARDEN
Bay
LOW DRIVE
Big Elm
BISHOP'S GATE
Contorted Willow
Chilean Firetree (Embothrium family)
Juniper
Balsam Poplar
Walnut
Irish Yew
Blue Cedar
Crimson King
Cryptomeria (Japanese Red Cedar)
Cedar
Turkey Oak

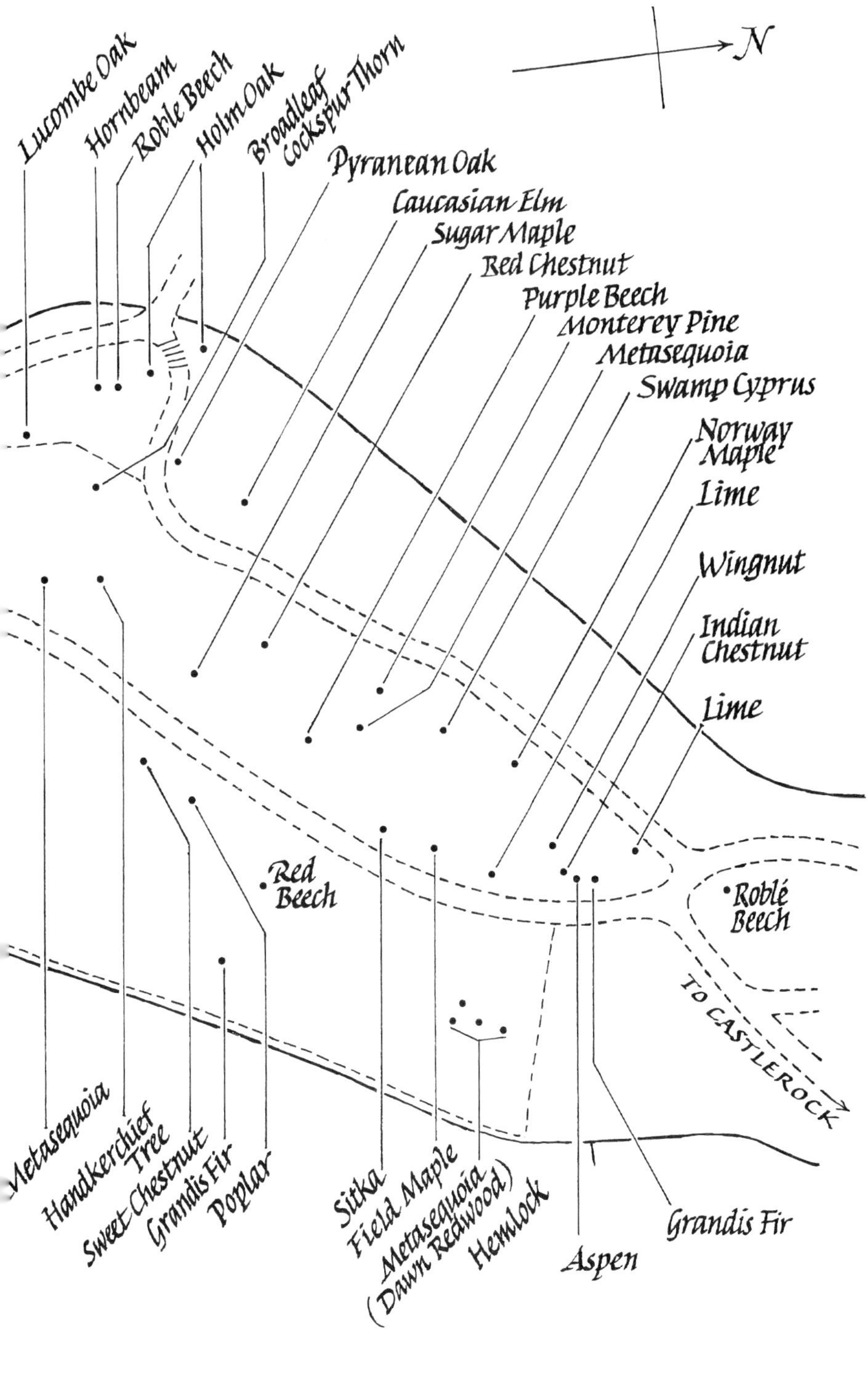
N
Lucombe Oak
Hornbeam
Roble Beech
Holm Oak
Broadleaf Cockspur Thorn
Pyranean Oak
Caucasian Elm
Sugar Maple
Red Chestnut
Purple Beech
Monterey Pine
Metasequoia
Swamp Cyprus
Norway Maple
Lime
Wingnut
Indian Chestnut
Lime
Roblé Beech
Red Beech
TO CASTLEROCK
Metasequoia
Handkerchief Tree
Sweet Chestnut
Grandis Fir
Poplar
Sitka
Field Maple
Metasequoia (Dawn Redwood)
Hemlock
Aspen
Grandis Fir

A selection of Downhill gardeners: (above) Mr Lines with his wife and family, (right) Bob Moore in the walled garden, and (below right) Miss Jan Eccles, National Trust warden from 1962 to 1994.

With the change of taste towards the end of the nineteenth century, the grounds may have been altered too, from providing a 'picturesque' adjunct to an episcopal palace to catering for the needs of the Victorian sportsman; pheasant coverts rather than ornamental park. The walled garden may well have received its heated glass-houses at this date; local people recall times when one could buy peaches from the Downhill gardens. Ajoining the fruit garden was the rose garden (now largely occupied by the car park) which would have supplied the Castle with fresh flowers. In 1910, a bog garden, originally called 'Lady Bruce's Garden', was created by the head gardener, Mr Lines, behind the bridge at the Bishop's Gate.

Cub Cadet

Primulas

The present bog garden was restored in the early 1960s and displays a wealth of naturalised primulas. Downhill violets are remembered as growing profusely on the steep bank from the Lion Gate towards the strand, but they were destroyed or died out when the main road was widened in 1982 (souvenir mugs with 'Downhill Violets' on them are also remembered). The glen contains a number of interesting trees apart from those mentioned, including: aspen, bay, whitebark birch, swamp cypress, crimson king, cryptomeria, eucalyptus, Caucasian elm, gingko, handkerchief tree, holly, hornbeam, liquidambar, juniper, maple, metasequoia, Pyrenean oak, plane, poplar, tulip tree, walnut and wingnut. In the Forestry part of the glen stands a huge sitka spruce, estimated to be 136 feet (41.5 metres) tall, though at the time of writing now sadly dying.

Birdlife

DOWNHILL teems with birdlife. Most visitors will know and recognise the common song birds and sea birds, and anyone who walks by the fishponds in Portvantage Glen will be delighted by the usual flocks of ducks – as tame as any in a city park – as well as by the coots, moorhen and occasional heron. They will be lucky however to spot a dipper or even a kingfisher there, though both have been seen. Sometimes whooper swans overwinter there too. One of the most unusual sights in Portvantage must have been in the 1950s when mallard were recorded nesting in trees.

The collardove arrived at the end of the 1950s and has increased since as it has everywhere (rock doves too, like the city pigeon). Seabirds which have increased include kittywakes and the black guillemot, and fulmars have been seen since the 1920s. The gaudy but bad-mannered jay is now seen more frequently too. The kestrel has come also and in past times has even nested in Portvantage. Owls are occasionally noted, more usually the barn owl, but sometimes the rarer long-eared owl.

On the *valete* side of the bird population, the last woodcock was seen in the 1960s, though the bird was probably quite plentiful in the last century and no doubt would have appeared on the Castle's dining table in season. The corncrake too has not been heard in recent

Corncrake

years (1985) – its disappearance probably coinciding with the disappearance of oats and other grain crops from the fields around the Castle.

Lucky and keen-eyed visitors may spot a treecreeper in the Glen, or even the brighter-coloured crossbill. Perhaps the rarest and most exotic bird to have been seen in Downhill was a Hoopoe which came for about a week in the early 1960s.

Peter Scott

Not everyone realises that there is a stronger link than that of bird-watching between Downhill and the celebrated naturalist and artist Peter Scott, in that his mother was Kathleen Bruce and thus his great-grandfather was Sir James Robertson Bruce, the second baronet Downhill. In 1987 Sir Peter visited Coleraine University but unfortunately was too pressed for time to visit his mother's ancestral home. Sir Peter died in 1990.

Folk legend and the supernatural

THERE ARE so many forts and caves in the area dating from both prehistory and from Celtic times that it would be surprising if there were not a body of local supernatural legend. From the south-facing drawing room of Downhill Castle could easily be seen the Giant's Sconce on the horizon. This fanciful name was given to a Celtic fort which originally was known as the *Dun Ceithern* or Ceithern's fort. Ceithern was a descendant of the Irish king Niall and was contemporary with St Patrick (Ceithern also means a group of soldiers). However there was a period when the idea of a land of giants was more attractive than factual history, so accordingly there is also a Giant's Grave and a Giant's Seat nearby – all much more fun for the boys and girls of Articlave who traditionally went to the Sconce for school outings. The word 'sconce' which might usually be applied to a candlestick is not totally inappropriate, as the place had also once been used for a signal beacon.

On the other side of the Castle, looking down from the Temple can be seen the outcrop of rock known as the Tether Stack or sometimes the Tether Stake (*Backaun na boe* in Irish). Various versions of the same local story exist concerning this rock; in its simplest form it is related that during a time of famine in the land, a miraculous cow, whose endless supply of milk was sustaining the people, was kept tethered there. As long as she was not milked dry the supply would continue. Unfortunately this was just what happened, the villains being strangers who came at night and milked her secretly. Dunboe means fort of the cow.

Linking the distant past with the Bishop's time is a splendid story concerning the 'iron chest of St Columcille'. Again there are variations, but that of the Field Survey of 1835 comes to us with the authority of John Wisely and David McBlain. Tradition held that an iron chest kept in the Temple contained old books and manuscripts, prophesies of St 'Columkiln', and could be opened only by a man not born (like Shakespeare's Macduff) who rode on a white horse with no black hair that similarly had never been foaled. The Bishop who was supposed to have been born by cæsarean section (this is a little unlikely as it was a rarely performed operation in the eighteenth

The Tether Stack

century and was then often fatal to the mother) managed to acquire the appropriate horse and proceeded to open the chest. The contents of the box are never minutely described – though according to one version it was full of serpents which then mysteriously disappeared – but a short perusal caused the Bishop to go very pale and to shut it up again very smartly. 'The consequence was that the Bishop could not sleep two nights in one house and from the disquiet state of his mind fled to Rome where it is said he died a Papist and in a miserable state'. The chest was apparently sent to Derry.

A place so full of history as Downhill must of necessity have a fair number of ghosts. It is said that a ghost coach comes from the Castle at midnight, and also that a lady in blue is to be seen at times in the Glen. The ghost with the most recent history must be that of the supposed murdered butler (see page 147) who it is thought is in possession of the whereabouts of hidden treasure, and will reveal it to anyone courageous enough to follow him. Buried treasure and the supernatural traditionally quite often go together; the 1835 Survey mentions a certain James McLaughlin who, having dreamt three times of treasure buried under a standing stone at Dunalis in 1800, proceeded to dig for it, only to have the stone fall and break his thigh.

A mystery which will perhaps abide as long as any concerns the existence of the 'Ghost Brae'. The working accounts for the Bishop's estates in 1773 include several references to planting or 'digging pitts for Planting' in a place variously named as 'Ghost Brae', 'Gohost Bray', 'the Gost Brea' and 'Ghost meadow'. Even today it is unclear which piece of land is meant here, and whether it took its name from being genuinely haunted, or whether from a corruption of the Irish word 'gort', a tilled field, is also not known.

George, Lord Bristol, was sometimes supposed to have died in consequence of a fall from his horse, it having been frightened by a white hare; since when the sighting of a white hare is thought to presage a death in the family of the Bruces.

Shipwrecks

THE NORTH COAST can be particularly inhospitable to seafarers, as the remains of the Spanish Armada found in 1588, and as witnessed by the discovery of the treasures from the *Gerona*. Of more recent shipwrecks, a local legend speaks of a convict ship which in the Bishop's time anchored off Portvantage to await a fair wind and tide to continue her voyage from Derry to Australia. The officers were apparently bidden to dine at Downhill and while so engaged the weather changed suddenly and the vessel went on the rocks. A small brass cannon retained by the Portrush Yacht Club is said to have been salvaged from her. Rather better documented was the wreck of the Norwegian Brig *Hilding*. She was bound for the West Indies from Glasgow and foundered at 'the entrance to Londonderry river on January 25, 1878.' The skipper of the brig, Berthiius Jargensen perished and his gravestone can be seen in Tamlaghtard graveyard. However there were survivors from this ship, and some of them were looked after at the Castle as guests of Sir Hervey Bruce. As late as 1958 members of survivors' families were trying to contact both the descendants of the volunteer rescue crew and the Bruces. Less fortunate were the seamen of the *Trader*, bound from Galway for London which went down by the Castle rock in November of 1826. Eight of these unlucky ones are buried in the graveyard of St Paul's, Articlave. A local ballad was written – in a vein reminiscent of McGonagall – shortly after the tragedy:

'Our ship was good and she might have well stood,
    although tremendous winds did blow,
When a sudden shock upon a rock,
    it caused our helm off to go.'

The Downhill Harp

IN GUINNESS'S BREWERY in Dublin there is a very handsome harp known as the Downhill Harp. This was formerly in the possession of the Bruce family, having been given to Henry Hervey Bruce, the third baronet, by its owner Denis or Donnehadh O'Hempsey (Hampsy) when on his deathbed. (The dates here are very uncertain, some sources giving O'Hempsey's death as 1870, others at 1807!) He had lived at Benone, Magilligan, in a cottage given by the Bishop, and had been a celebrated performer on the instrument. The harp itself had a fairly distinguished history, having been played before Bonnie Prince Charlie in 1745. It had been made by Cormac O'Kelly in 1702, as testified by some verses inscribed on the side of its soundbox:

> 'In the time of Noah I was green
> . . . his flood I have not been seen
> vntil 17 hundred and 02 I was fovnd
> by C R Kely vndergrovnd
> He raised me up to that degree
> Qveen of mvsick yv may call me'

The rhymes would suggest that bog oak might feature in its construction. It is unlikely that Guinness modelled its harp symbol on the Downhill instrument since the brewery did not acquire it until long after the familiar bottle label had been well established.

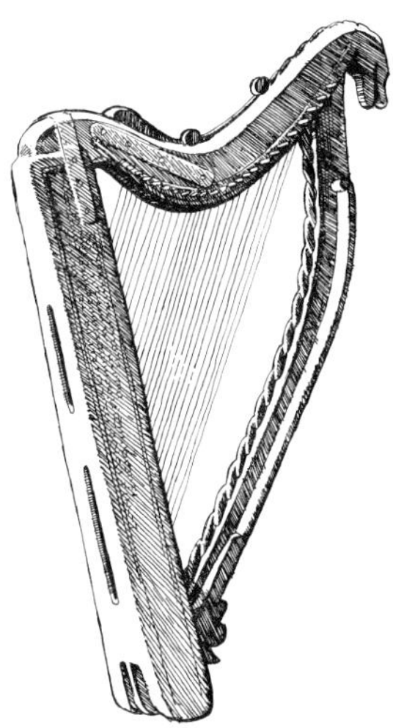

The Downhill harp

Hezlett House

HEZLETT HOUSE is very much older than Downhill Castle, and despite being a much humbler building, has survived very much better than its grander neighbour. It has been estimated that it was built in about 1691, and was originally a farmhouse or possibly a rectory. Certainly it was used by the rector Roger fford at the end of the seventeenth century, and by four other rectors in succession after until 1761 when it was taken over by Isaac Hezlett. The Hezletts lived in the house continuously almost up to the time when it was acquired by the National Trust in 1976.

The Trust's interest in the house was largely due to its curious construction which, although by no means unique in the area, was then more common in England than in Ireland. Originally the house was constructed in a framework of five timber 'crucks', curved and jointed pieces of oak which formed uprights and rafters rather in the manner of the ribs of an upside down boat. These timbers sat on a base of rocks and the spaces in between filled with thick walls formed from roughcast with an infill of clay and sand. The roof was thatched with flax. When Isaac Hezlett married in 1823 he extended the house by two more bays to the south so that his mother and sisters could remain under the same roof as the family expanded. The walled garden in front of the house was only created at the end of the last century, having been a farm courtyard until then.

The National Trust have left one room quite open from floor to roof so that the construction of the building can be seen by visitors. Today the house has relatively fresh thatch; when it was rethatched in 1983 it was discovered that no old thatch had ever been removed in the house's entire existence and the accumulated weight of seven foot of straw was causing the timber frames to sag dangerously. More recently one of the crucks has had to be partly renewed and so successful has been the use of the traditional methods of cutting and fitting the wood that it is difficult to distinguish which timbers are modern and which 300 years old.

Hezlett House impressed visitors in the past as much as it does now. In 1758 a distinguished visitor was one Mrs Delany, who said of the occasion, 'The cabin is a lowly one, but elegantly neat, and decorated in a pretty taste with some very fine pieces of china: very good tea, very good supper, and *above all* very good instructive conversation.'

Mrs Mary Delany was an Englishwoman who was married to the Dean of Down and lived in Glasnevin and Downpatrick. Her chief claim to fame was in her extraordinary flower collages, or 'papermosaicks' as she called them. These were the most delicate and accurate pictures made up from cut coloured paper pasted on to a plain background. Sometimes a flower might be made up of over a hundred fragments of paper. Some ten albums as well as many single sheets of Mrs Delany's work now reside in the print room of the British Museum, comprising some 1,000 examples of flowers. It would be pleasant to think that some of her pictures may have been inspired by specimens seen at Downhill.

A 'papermosaick' by Mrs Delany, *Bombax ceiba.*

The Railway

THE RAILWAY LINK between Coleraine and Londonderry was built in the middle of the last century and to a certain extent brought change to the area and the lives of those living there. The development of Castlerock was itself largely due to the arrival of the railway, although it never grew to rival Portstewart or Portrush as a resort, much as the promoters of the time would have wished. The Railway Company actually offered subsidised travel to people contemplating building or settling in Castlerock. The Bruce family also encouraged the development of the town and it is significant that the station was designed by the architect John Lanyon who, in addition to designing other stops on the line (Magilligan Halt, Bellarena Station) was also responsible for remodelling Downhill Castle after the fire of 1851 (see p19).

The most spectacular part of the engineering work on the line must have been the cutting of the two tunnels through the cliffs on either side of Portvantage. At one time about 250 men were employed either on the tunnels themselves or in related work such as making bricks for the interior walls. Explosives were used twice to break up the very tough volcanic rock. A geological report of the period noted that some of the material resembled that of the Giant's Causeway. The 'Great Blast' of 1846 used some 3,600 lbs of powder and was advertised as a spectacle by the company, which also provided a candlelit dinner in the tunnel for some 500 people later. It must be a matter of speculation as to how much Sir Hervey Bruce worried about these huge explosions being set off virtually underneath the Mussenden Temple! The first train to carry passengers went through the tunnels in July 1853.

Acknowledgments

The Editors would like to thank all the many people who have helped with encouragement and information in the compilation of this 'scrapbook'. It would be difficult to name everyone concerned but particular thanks should go to: Verily Anderson Paget, Beryl Bruce, Jim Chestnutt, Dixie Dean, Grace Fraser, Miranda Harrison, Alison McCaughan, Peter Mulholland, Peter Rankin, Philip Watson.

The Photographs in this book have been reproduced by kind permission of the following sources:

Verily Anderson Paget. Page 162
The British Museum, Prints and Drawings Department. Page 185
J. Chestnutt. Pages 10, 20, 21, 22, 52, 92, 153, 155
Country Life Picture Library. Page 91
J. A. K. Dean. Page 34
A. F. Kersting. Pages 68, 80, 109
Raymond Mander & Joe Mitchenson Theatre Collection. Page 157
National Gallery of Ireland, Dublin. Page 75
National Portrait Gallery, London. Pages 77, 123
National Trust Photographic Library. Pages 70, 110, 126, 129, 139
Sir John Soane's Museum, London. Pages 29, 30, 35
Dr B. M. Walker, Director of The Institute of Irish Studies, Queen's University, Belfast. Page 44
The Witt Library, Courtauld Institute of Art, London. Page 108
The Ulster Museum, Belfast. Pages 36, 60, 62, 143

All line Illustrations/maps supplied by Printing Ideas & Graphics

Bibliography

Anderson, Verily. *The Last of the Eccentrics, A Life of Rosslyn Bruce*, Hodder and Stoughton, London 1972.
H.J. Bruce. *Silken Dalliance*, London 1946.
— *Thirty Dozen Moons*, London 1949.
Childe-Pemberton, W. S. *The Earl Bishop*, 2 vols, London 1924.
Day, Angélique, and Patrick McWilliams (editors). *Ordnance Survey Memoirs of Ireland, vol II, Belfast* 1991.
Erskine, David. *Augustus Hervey's Journal*, London 1953.
Foster, Vere. *The Two Duchesses*, London 1898.
Fothergill, Brian. *The Mitred Earl, An Eighteenth-Century Eccentric*, London 1974.
Gallagher, Lyn, and Dick Rogers. *Castle, Coast and Cottage*, Belfast 1986.
Girvan, W. D. *Buildings of North Derry*, Belfast 1975.
Green, E. R. R. 'Downhill Castle, County Derry, Northern Ireland', *Country Life* 1950.
Joyce, P. W. *Irish Names of Places*, Dublin 1891.
Lecky, W. E. H. *A History of Ireland in the Eighteenth Century*, 2 vols, London 1902.
McCaughan, Alison. *Heath, Hearth and Home*, Coleraine 1988.
Mullin, J. E. *The Causeway Coast*, Belfast 1974.
Rankin, Peter. *Irish Building Ventures of the Earl Bishop of Derry*, Belfast 1972.
— 'Downhill, Co. Derry', *Country Life*, July 1971.

Scholars seeking further historical detail would do well to consult the 'Hervey-Bruce Papers', a large body of contemporary documents held by the Public Record Office of Northern Ireland, Belfast; and also 'Downhill Demesne', an exhaustive study carried out by Terence Reeves-Smyth for the National Trust in 1992.

Index

Italic figures indicate pictures